Hope Over Pain
CRPS / RSD
Awareness & Research Cookbook
2011

Samantha M Adcock, Editor

Let's Get Hoppin'
  This Pain Needs Stoppin'

DEDICATION

On behalf of everyone at Hope Over Pain, we want to thank all of you for your support and encouragement.

The First Annual Hope Over Pain CRPS/RSD Awareness & Research Cookbook was possible only through the tireless support of so many within our community.

We thank you for opening your hearts and your secret family cookbooks to provide tasty & tantalizing recipes all with the hope of raising awareness. While enjoying all the recipes and tips and tricks for cooking, we have also included CRPS factoids, poetry, narratives and resources throughout this amazing cookbook. We have also included ways to minimize the stress on our systems and for those unfamiliar with our world, a gentle introduction is included, a chance to glimpse into the life of a CRPS survivor.

Special thanks to the researchers, advocacy groups along with our family and friends who have helped with this cookbook. Many of these people have been placed along the path we've been redirected onto and while we don't have the choice of walking away, the lives of those who are closest to us are just as impacted by our condition as ours are, just in a different way. It takes a very strong person to stand by us. We do appreciate it, no matter how it may seem on our darkest days.

We did NOT choose to have CRPS/RSD, but we CAN choose how we live with it.

We choose Hope Over Pain!

"There are moments in your life that makes you and sets the course of who you are. Sometimes they are little, subtle moments. Sometimes they are Big moments you never saw coming. No one asks for their life to change, but it does. It's what you do afterwards that counts...That's when you find out who you are." Cyndi Wilson Ellis

In Loving Memory of Shirley Ann Barts 12/20/30 - 07/05/2011
"Rest in Peace Mom. Shine your light upon us from above as you always did. Thank you for being such a wonderful mother and parent, role model, friend. I know you always did the best you could and I will continue to live by your example and do the best I can with what I have....I thank the Lord for you and time he gave us with you. I Will Love You Forever, and Like You For Always, My Mother You Will Always Be." Sharon Romensko.

THE MONSTER INSIDE ME

Tanner Saunders© 2011

I was crouched and waiting for it.

The ball came in so unbelievably fast.

Next was the sound of the ball being tipped off of a bat.

Unbelievably, the ball made contact with my foot!

I picked it up and immediately threw it to second.

Coach Rick yelled, "You're out!" "Nice throw, Tanner!"

Next, Brandon hit the ball, and it was a homerun!

He yelled to me, "We won!"

What I didn't know, was that ball changed my life forever. I wasn't

prepared for the devastating words from my doctor.

"You can't play baseball, football, or any other contact sports," he

said.

I felt numb, that is, until the pain set in two days later.

The next few days were a nightmare.

The pain in my foot was unbearable.

Nothing would give me relief.

The x-rays came back negative, but they still put a cast on my left

foot.

When the burning started, the cast was taken off because my foot

felt like it was on fire.

The relief was tremendous, but it did not last long.

After much testing at the hospital, my doctor delivered the verdict

that changed my life forever.

"Tanner," you have RSD."

What is Reflex Sympathetic Dystrophy?

Unfortunately, I was soon to find out.

It's like a fire igniting inside my body that just keeps burning and

burning.

It means horrible insomnia because the pain is so bad.

It means a short attention span because of the many meds I take.

It means missing school because it's too painful to sit in one place

and concentrate.

It means having "supporters" but not a lot of "friends".

It means not doing a lot of fun things that normal high schoolers

get to do.

It means that spending time in a hospital is now a normal part of my life.

It means never being able to plan anything, because I never know if I will be feeling painless or painful.

It means being upset when the burning travels to another part of my body.

It means living with an incontrollable monster in my body forever. There is no cure for the monster, RSD.

Who could ever predict that an innocent hit in the foot could destroy a young person's life?

Who could ever know how devastating and incurable RSD could be?

Who could ever imagine what the rest of my life will be like while this unwanted monster lives in me?

Dealing with problems is part of everyday life.

Living with the monster, RSD, is mine.

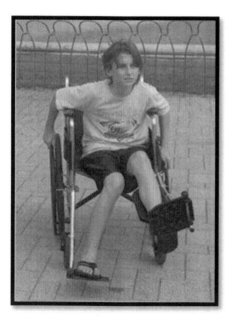

CONTENTS

Special Dietary Needs

Many diseases and conditions, including allergies, and/or your family history, can require changes in your diet to keep you feeling well and in good health.

We've included many tasty recipes for a variety of Special Dietary Needs.

Watch for these icons to help you find a variety of tempting new dishes that are sure to delight your tastebuds:

Special Dietary Needs

Recipes High in Fiber

Living with the Demon Monster (RSD/CRPS)

Jerry Paul Pond© 2011

Now we find our life is a big game that always is challenging us, especially when some of your family, friends, doctors, nurses, and your work place don't believe you could be feeling all the pain you have described.

That is why I am telling you it's important that you share information about this crazy disease called RSD/ CRPS with those close to you. To help them understand what you're experiencing daily because, for us, every day is different. Education, support groups, and talking are our life lines.

We have to try to take care of our physical and mental health the best we can by maintain some kind of normal daily activities when we can. Pace yourself and when you feel the need to lay down, lay down. Try hard to stay connected with your family and friends. If you had hobbies continue the ones that you enjoy and can do.

Try learning relaxation techniques, and try hard learning way to reduce your stress. Support groups and Face book friends help a lot..

ACKNOWLEDGMENTS

The author's references to various brand-name products and services are for information purposes only and are not intended to suggest endorsement or sponsorship of the author or her book by any company, organization, or owner of any brand.

Our Contributors, Supporters and Volunteers: Cyndi Wilson Ellis, Lisa VanOostwaard, Lesle McGuffey, Jerry Pond, Jill Milner, Diane Jones, Debra Schueller Robinson, Bernadette Chew, Christine La Duke Beausoleil, Peggy Lindsay, Kristin Lathrop, Sonja Leigh Comb, Trudy Apicella, Sara Willy Timmons, Susan James Massengill, Tammy Broselow, Patty Burke, Maria Anne Tripp Martinez, Sandra Martineau, Kim Dunning-Powell, Stephanie Maberry, Kim Robinson Fox, Brenda Lewis, Marla D Brownfield, Dionetta Hudzinski, Grace W. Allen, Kelly Allen, Kerry Adams, Karen Slater, Nettan Svensson,Karol Patras, Laurie Paul, Joy Horner, Dawn Clark, Grecia Howard, Tracy Meyer Morrow, Tonya Brobeck, Ann Beauregard, Jane Gonzales, Sharon Romenesko, Patty Burke, Laurie Paul, Tiffany Mazza, Wendy Marsh, Jen Dwyer, Joy Horner, Kellye Van Dyke, Brooke Nelson, Suzanne Stewart, Jennifer L. Brande, Wendy Marsh, Amy Kimmel, Kathy Crews, Erin Dasher, Maureen McNamara, Cyndi Wilson Ellis, Tammy Broselow, Donna Topock, Cathe Satterthwaite, Jill Milner, Diane Jones, Zoe Blatchley, Mary-Ann Hankins, Karl Adcock, Sean Samitt, Bonnie Barclay-Koch, Jerry Paul Pond, Tanner Saunders, Amber Wiseman, Isabel - RSD/CRPS Research and Developments, and special thanks to my sister Sandra Kay Burgess who generously provided Alaska glacier photos that form the background in many of our CRPS Awareness Graphics.

U.S. National Library of Medicine, CRPS/ESD Awareness World of Fire & Ice Graphics, Here to Help RSD, Logo courtesy of Kompass Health Associates, New Zealand; RSD Sisters, RSD Painfree., RSD/CRPS Research and Developement

INTRODUCTION

Hope Over Pain is an all-volunteer organization comprised of individuals whose lives have been impacted by one or more debilitating chronic pain conditions. Our mission is to reduce and eliminate barriers preventing patients with Chronic and Intractable Pain conditions such as Complex Regional Pain Syndrome (CRPS) formerly known as Reflex Sympathetic Dystrophy (RSD), Fibromyalgia, Lupus & Multiple Sclerosis (MS) from achieving effective Pain Management.

Complex regional pain syndrome (CRPS) is a rare, poorly understood chronic pain syndrome affecting between 200,000 and 1.2 million Americans and over 5 million worldwide. Typical features include dramatic changes in the color and temperature of the skin over the affected limb or body part, accompanied by intense burning pain, skin sensitivity, sweating, and swelling. Although many advances in medicine have occurred over the past 150 years, treatments for this condition are not widely effective for patients.

The hope of HOP (Hope Over Pain- pronounced "hope") is to provide a voice to both the public and medical community about our disease, to raise awareness and to provide a community that patients can turn to for support and healing.

For those living with Complex Regional Pain Syndrome preparing meals for the family or even just for oneself can become a difficult and painful challenge. In an effort to raise awareness, HOP presents its First Annual Awareness Cookbook

APPETIZERS, DIPS
&
BEVERAGES

SEVEN LAYER MEXICAN DIP

Debra Schueller Robinson

Select ingredient quantities based on number of people being severed & personal preference. You can't go wrong with this recipe.

Guacamole (Fresh or already prepared)
Refried Beans or black Beans
2 cups Sour Cream
1 package Taco seasoning
Thinly diced onions
Chopped fresh tomatoes
Sliced black olives
Mexico shredded Cheese

1. Mix 16 oz or two cups of Sour cream with 1 package of Taco seasoning.
2. Chop tomatoes and thinly dice onions.
3. Cook refried beans or black beans.
4. Layer the ingredients as shown above, with the top ingredient being on the bottom of the pan.
5. Serve with tortilla chips to dip.

Easy Dip

Christine La Duke Beausoleil

1 jar of Cheez Whiz™

16 oz of cottage cheese

1. Empty Cheez Whiz™ into a medium sized bowl & stir until softened
2. Add cottage cheese, stirring lightly until mixed completely.

This dip can be used with just about any veggies or crackers. My girls who didn't want to try plain cottage cheese ate this & loved it!

Hot Artichoke Dip

Bernadette Chew   Chico, CA

Canned Artichoke

Diced green chilies (canned)

1 cup Mayo

1. Mix all ingredients together
2. Heat and serve with Tortilla Chips

CREAM CHEESE AVOCADO SPREAD

Samantha Adcock   Shiloh, NC

1   Ripe avocado

1   3oz package cream cheese (softened)

1 1/2   teaspoon lemon juice

2 teaspoon   sherry

1. Peel avocados & mash pulp in small bowl
2. Combine remaining ingredients in food processor
3. Add avocado to cream cheese mixture, and blend thoroughly
4. Serve with mini rye hors d'oeuvre slices, with whole grain crackers

HOT PEPPERONI DIP

Paulette Anderson   PA

Monongahela Valley RSD Support Group of SW, Pa

1 pkg sliced pepperoni

2 pkg. Philadelphia® cream cheese

1 can cream of celery soup

1. Chop/dice pkg of pepperoni.
2. Place all ingredients together in crock pot.
3. Cook for 2-3 hours, stir occasionally.
4. Serve with Triscuits®, Baguettes, etc.

SHRIMPLY DELIGHTFUL DIP

Samantha Adcock   Shiloh, NC

This is a crowd pleaser & one of the simplest dishes could ever make. It's a personal favorite of mine for potlucks, family gatherings & office parties. It can be assembled on site In less than five minutes, and there are never any leftovers to carry home.

Use an attractive disposable container & there won't even be any washing up afterwards!

1   8 oz. block cream cheese
1   4 oz. can tiny shrimp (drained & rinsed)
Cocktail sauce (recipe below or small jar)

1. Place block of cream in the center of oval or round dish that is twice its size.
2. Pour cocktail sauce over cream cheese & allow it to cover open area on plate.

3. Sprinkle the shrimp over the top of the cream cheese and scattering in the sauce surrounding it.
4. Serve with your choice crackers

SHRIMP COCKTAIL SAUCE

1/2 c catsup

2 Tablespoons lemon juice

2 table spoon grated onion

2 table spoons mayonnaise or salad dressing

1 teaspoon garlic salt

1 teaspoon Worcestershire sauce

1/4 teaspoon salt

Dash pepper

1. Combine all ingredients & Chill

TRIPLE SPICY CHEESE FRIES

Sonja Leigh Comb   KY

1   1 ½ lb frozen French fries
1/2 block Velveeta ®cheese (cut in 1 inch cubes)
1   can of Pace® Chunky Salsa mild *'trust me you do not want to go any hotter or you'll regret it'*

2   cans of your favorite chili

1   jar of Mt. Olive® jalapenos

1   Preheat oven per package directions.
    - While your oven is preheating, gather all ingredients, and 2 medium, microwave safe mixing bowls.
    - Open fries and evenly distribute in a deep casserole dish (*for easy clean up use comparable size disposable foil pan*) .
2   Once oven is preheated, place pan in oven checking every 10 – 15 minutes for 30 minutes, stir as needed. Continue checking every 5 minutes until 7 minutes remain.
3   While fries are cooking cut cheese into 1 inch cubes.
4   Combine cheese cubes & 1/2 to 3/4 jar of salsa *according to taste* in bowl & microwave on high for 4 minutes, or until cheese is completely melted. **Pause & stir in one minute intervals to prevent scorching**
5   Heat chili in microwave 3 minutes or until hot.
6   Remove fries from oven, & top with heated chili. Spread with spoon to cover evenly.
7   Add cheese mixture on top of chili, spread until evenly covered.
8   Layer your jalapenos on top in rows using around 1/2 jar or less according to your taste
9   Let stand about 20 minutes or until it's a little cooler.

Yields about 10-15 servings

This is good and easy to make for football or basketball games and makes a great super bowl party food. Also kids usually really like it!

JALAPEÑO POPPER DIP

Trudy Apicella   Oakville, CT

This dip taste exactly like the jalapeño poppers that you get in the restaurant. Serve with tortilla chips or crackers. It is very easy and fast to make and everyone that has it loves it

2   8 ounce packages of cream cheese softened
1   cup of mayonnaise
2   4 ounce cans of chopped green chilies
2   ounces of jalapenos drained and chopped   you can add more to taste
½   cup of parmesan cheese   more or less depending on your taste

1. Mix the cream cheese and mayonnaise in a bowl
2. add the chilies and jalapeños
3. sprinkle cheese on top
4. cook in microwavable dish for 2 minutes stir and cook 2 minutes or more if needed.

THREE WAY AVOCADO DIP

Lian   Australia

1 pkg. soft Philadelphia cheese.
1 ripe avocado
1 jar salsa sauce (mild or hot)

1. Break cheese up slightly with a fork. Then put it in the bottom of a large breakfast bowl or in to 4 to 6 small individual bowl.
2. Mash the avocado and put on top of the soft cheese.
3. Top with all of the salsa sauce making sure all avocado is covered.
4. You can serve it now or put it in the fridge for up to 2 days as long as all avocado is covered with the salsa sauce.
5. serve with crackers

My mother's 3 way dip can be used as an entree or a party dip depending on how you serve it. I used this as an entree in small dishes so each had their own, for Christmas day 2010. They loved it!

SPICY CHICKEN WING DIP

Kristin Lathrop

16 oz. Cream cheese (2 standard packages)

8 oz. Sharp Cheese (grated) 2 cups

12 oz. hot sauce bottle (your favorite kind)

8 oz. Blue Cheese Dressing.

1 lg chicken breast (cooked and shredded or diced into tiny pieces)

1. Mix all ingredients in a 9X13 pan.
2. Bake at 350 degrees for 25 to 30 min.
3. Serve warm w/ favorite dip chips (ex. corn chip scoops) for less spicy flavor only use 1/2 bottle of hot sauce.

PICKLE AND PASTRAMI

Sara Willy Timmons   Saukville, WI

2 pkg of Buddy® pastrami

7 large dried off pickles

8 oz cream cheese

1 tablespoon Worcestershire

Dash powdered garlic

Add mayo to make spreadable

1. Take 2 squares of Buddy pastrami
2. Spread cream cheese mixture on pastrami
3. Roll meat around pickle
4. Refrigerate then slice before serving.

DAIRY-FREE HERB DIP

Amber Wiseman   OH

Lactose intolerant, but want to enjoy dip with your chips, pretzels, or vegetables?

No need to skip on the taste, you can have what you want and avoid the dairy. I usually end up just going through the spice rack and adding what sounds good and what we have on hand.

1 package silk

soft Tofu

½ c. chopped parsley

2 Tablespoon mayonnaise or soy-naise

2 Tablespoon fresh lemon juice

2 Tablespoon chopped green olives

2 finely chopped green onions or chive

1 clove garlic

1 teaspoon Worcestershire sauce

½ teaspoon table salt

½ teaspoon thyme

Throw all ingredients into a food processor until well blended.

CRAB SPREAD

Samantha Adcock   Shiloh, NC

14 oz of crab or imitation crab meat

1/2 cup mayonnaise

2 t horseradish

2 T lemon juice

2 T minced green onions

1 t salt

1/4 t pepper

1. Combine all ingredients,
2. Cover & chill. Serve with crackers.

EASY SOUTHERN PIMENTO CHEESE SPREAD

Peggy Lindsay   Louisburg , NC

10 ozs. finely shredded sharp cheddar cheese

2oz. jar of pimentos plus juice

1/2 tsp. mustard

1 1/4 cup good mayonnaise

dashes of Tobasco® sauce (more for spicier)

2 tbsp. grated onion

Mix all & spread (or just eat!)

CUCUMBER YOGURT DIP

Samantha Adcock   Shiloh, NC

  1 large cucumber

  2 cups plain yogurt, low-fat

  ½ cup sour cream, non-fat

  1 tablespoon lemon juice

  1 tablespoon fresh dill

  1 garlic clove, chopped

1   Peel, seed, and grate one cucumber.
2   Mix grated cucumber, yogurt, sour cream, lemon juice,
    dill, and garlic in a serving bowl.
3   Chill for 1 hour before serving.

FRUIT DIP

Amber Wiseman   OH

Very easy to make and delicious to eat! You can try this
with any sort of fruit. You can also make a giant sugar
cookie, add fruit dip, and then top it with your favorite fruit
to make a fruit pizza.

  Cream Cheese
  Marshmallow Cream
  Fruit

1. Combine equal parts cream cheese and marshmallow cream, mix well.
2. Dip fruit. Enjoy!

MANGO SALSA

Samantha Adcock   Shiloh, NC

2 cups diced tomatoes

1 1/2 cups diced mango

1/2 cup diced onion

1 teaspoon white sugar

1/2 cup chopped fresh cilantro

2 tablespoons fresh lime juice

1 tablespoon cider vinegar

1/2 teaspoon salt

1/2 teaspoon black pepper

2 cloves garlic, minced

1. Stir the tomatoes, mango, onion, sugar, cilantro, lime juice, cider vinegar, salt, pepper, and garlic together in a bowl
2. Refrigerate 1 hour before serving.

FROZEN FRUIT SLUSHIE

Tammy Broselow   Las Vegas, NV

Any frozen berries / fruits you like (must be frozen to
make the slushie)
1 fresh banana
Any juice (apple definitely works)
Optional fresh fruit

1 Place all ingredients together in a blender
2 Mix on high
3 Serve chilled with a spoon or straw

BANANA MILKSHAKE

Samantha Adcock   Shiloh, NC

2 cups vanilla ice cream

1 small Banana

1/2   cup milk

1/2 teaspoon pure vanilla extract (not imitation)

1. Place 2 glasses in freezer to chill
2. Combine ice cream, banana, vanilla and milk in blender.
3. Blend until smooth, if you prefer your shake a little add
   a bit more milk.
4. Serve immediately in tall chilled glass

MAGICAL MALTED MILKSHAKE

Sonja Leigh Comb   KY

1 cup of vanilla ice cream

6 tablespoons of chocolate syrup (or more depending on your taste, but don't add more than 10 or it loses the malt effect)

1 pack of SwissMiss® or Nestle® hot cocoa or hot chocolate,

3/4 cup of milk

1 Hershey® milk chocolate candy bar

ReadyWhip® whipped topping

1 Marachino cherry (optional)

1. Combine first 4 ingredients in a blender.
2. Blend until smooth and all ingredients are thoroughly combined
3. Remove from blender and place mixture in a chilled 16 oz glass (chill the glass for about 2-3 hours in the freezer before-hand)
4. Spray ReadyWhip® in a circular motion on top of the mixture around the glass about 3-4 times making a pretty big layer
5. Break up half of the Hershey candy bar (and eat the other half we deserve some chocolate every now and then) into small pieces about 1/4 or 1/8 inch (you don't want bigger than that)

6. Sprinkle the pieces of Hershey candy bar into the whipped topping (to make it look better you can place candy bar pieces all over the topping with your fingers)
7. (optional): place candied cherry on top in the middle of the whipped *topping*
8. Return to freezer for 30 to 45 minutes to refreeze, serve.

My friends absolutely love this and still don't know my secret to making the best milkshakes.

FUN DRINK

Maria Anne Tripp Martinez   San Antonio, TX

Guava Nectar
Ginger Ale
Ground Ginger

1. Fill a drinking cup with 1/3-1/2 Guava Nectar
2. Fill the other part with Ginger Ale
3. Add a sprinkle of ground ginger & stir

I have added other flavors of Nectar and been just as happy with the flavor.

FRUIT CUBES

Patty Burke   Florida

You can use cranberries, blueberries, raspberries, etc. Your choice and combinations.

1   Put berries or fruit of your choice into ice cube trays, add water.
2   With a toothpick, poke a small hole into each berry to release some of the juice as it freezes; place in freezer until frozen.

When you have or serve drinks; water, iced tea, whatever your choice, drop in fruit cubes for flavor and lots of vitamins and antioxidants.

Frozen cubes can also be thrown into blender when making blender drinks.

"Research studies have shown us that 500 mg Vitamin C taken daily (for 50 days) after injuries and surgeries, decreases the percentage of people developing CRPS by over 75%, this has been proven in multiple studies bearing similar results every time.."

Sandra Martineau
(CRPS/-RSD)
RSD/CRPS Research and Development

WASSAIL (HOT SPICED APPLE CIDER)

Samantha Adcock   Shiloh, NC

1 gal. apple cider

2 c. orange juice

1 c. lemon juice + 1/2 c. sugar (or use 1 sm. can frozen lemonade)

2 tsp. cinnamon

1 tsp. cloves

1 tsp. nutmeg

1   Mix ingredients and slowly bring to boil in large saucepan or pot. Boil for 1 minute.

2   Serve hot with sliced oranges floating in punch bowl.

CRPS can strike at any age and affects both men and women, although most experts agree that it is more common in young women. When diagnosed in children it is often diagnosed as Reflex Neurovascular Dystrophy (RND).

My RSD Prayer

Some days I don't even know which to pray for: the release of pain or the courage to go through it.

Sometimes I feel like I am surrounded by a dark heavy cloud. Not only is it around me, it is within me too. Help me to remember that no matter how dark the day, the sun is shining - I just can't see it now. I trust in your presence to bring light out of darkness, hope out of despair.

Having RSD/CRPS can be very frightening. It is having something inside of me that is against me. During this time of struggle help me to remember, God, that you are even more deeply within me. You are at my very center with your deep compassion.

I open myself to your healing energy and let it flow through my whole body and especially to the area needing most attention. At times I feel bound by pain and my physical limitations. But in many ways I do not have to be bound. I can be free to feel all of my feelings: love, fear, anger, sadness, joy. My love does not have to be bound either. I can send it, through my prayers, to any person in the world, and I'm sending it to the millions of people out there and the many children who are suffering with this disease.

Let your healing power flow through them from head to toe revitalizing them and giving them new hope.

 -Amen-
Lesle McGuffey©2011

The United States Department of Agriculture (USDA) recommends a total daily fiber intake of at least 2 - 30 grams of fiber with the majority coming from soluble fiber. Most of us hear it & see it marketed, but really don't understand what that means, or why it's important to us.

Flaxseed is now believed to be one of the most versatile and beneficial sources of fiber available. Packed with nutritional components that can play an important role in your diet, flaxseed can be added to cereals; breads; muffin, pancake and cookie mixes; smoothies; juices; applesauce; salads; casseroles; and meat loaf.

"Preliminary studies show that flaxseed may help fight everything from heart disease and diabetes to breast cancer."

By Elaine Magee, MPH, RD ~ WebMD.com

BREADS, GRAINS & FIBER

"Flaxseed is used for many conditions related to the gastrointestinal (GI) tract, including ongoing constipation, colon damage due to overuse of laxatives, diarrhea, inflammation of the lining of the large intestine (diverticulitis), irritable bowel syndrome (IBS) or irritable colon, sores in the lining of the large intestine (ulcerative colitis), inflammation of the lining of the stomach (gastritis), and inflammation of the small intestine (enteritis)." U.S. National Library of Medicine

SMOOTH MOVE MORNING CRUNCH

Samantha Adcock   Shiloh, NC

Gastrointestinal (GI) problems are one of the most common side effects associated with most medications prescribed to attempt to manage the symptoms of Complex Regional Pain Syndrome (CRPS).

This recipe can be easily adjusted to adapt to whichever GI problem is making its appearance. Increasing or decreasing the flaxseed as needed to return the system to normal function.

For the days that it's a challenge to manage any type of meal, this is a perfect solution. It's light but nutritious and easy to digest. Just eliminate the nuts on the days when it's difficult to eat anything, and remember to stay well hydrated.

1 Tbs ground Flaxseed

2 Tbs Chopped Walnuts (or other chopped nut)

1/2 C applesauce

3 Tbs Cream of Wheat

3/4 C water

1/2 tsp cinnamon

1/2 tsp brown sugar or sugar substitute

1/2 tsp Vanilla

1   Mix the 1st seven ingredients together in a bowl & microwave for 1 1/2 minutes.
2   When microwave is finished stir in the vanilla

The Flaxseed gives the dish a pleasant slight nutty flavor. It can be increased as needed to help keep the GI system moving smoothly. And, it tastes good enough to eat as a snack or even as a dessert.

YORKSHIRE PUDDING

Kim Dunning-Powell   United Kingdom

Traditional Serves 4

4oz/125g flour

1 egg

pinch of salt

1/2 pt - 10fl oz / 300 mil of milk or milk and water

Beef drippin or lard or oil [works best with drippings/lard]

1   Preheat the oven to 230C / 446 ºf
2   Put the flour and salt in a bowl and add the egg
3   Mix the flour and egg together and gradually add the milk
4   Whisk briskly until smooth
5   Put the dripping/lard/oil into a Yorkshire Pudding tin or square baking tin [shallow]

6   Place in the oven to warm oil or melt the dripping/lard
7   Pour in the mixture and return to the oven for 45 to 60 minutes.

Tip: the mixture is best made at least an hour before require and left to stand. Can be made the previous day, covered and placed in the refrigerator until required.

BANANA BREAD

Sara Willy Timmons   Saukville, WI

3 cups sugar

4 beaten eggs

2 tsp baking soda

pinch of salt

1 cup of milk

8 mashed bananas

4 cups of flour

1 tsp Vanilla

1   Mix all ingredients together with mixer.
2   Bake in 3 greased bread pans.
3   Bake at 325 for 50 – 60 minutes or until toothpick inserted into center of loaf comes out clean & dry

JACK-OF-ALL-TRADES BISCUITS

Amber Wiseman   OH

There are SO many things you can do with this recipe, try rolling it out, adding brown sugar and cinnamon rolling, and cutting for cinnamon rolls.

Add garlic, cheese, bacon, herbs, etc. for a huge variety of flavors. Try berries, baking chips, nuts, or cinnamon for a scone-like biscuit. Serve as a breakfast sandwich with egg and cheese, serve as gravy and biscuits (for any time of day), have them for breakfast or a snack with a little butter. Yum*!*

2 c. flour

4 t baking powder

½ t cream of tartar

1 tsp salt

½ c butter

½ c milk

1. Preheat oven to 475°.
2. Combine everything but butter and milk.
3. Cut in butter with a fork or pastry blender.
4. Slowly add milk until flour is moist (may need more or less than ½ c).

5. Roll and cut or just drop balls on a greased cookie sheet.

6. Bake for 10-12 minutes.

PULL APART BREAD

Stephanie Maberry   Souderton PA

3 pkgs. (12 oz. ea.) refrigerated biscuit dough
1 cup sugar
2 tsp. cinnamon
½ cup butter
1 cup packed light brown sugar
½ cup raisins
½ cup chopped nuts (optional)

1. Mix cinnamon and sugar in a Ziploc bag. Cut biscuits into quarters. Put 8 pieces into baggie at a time and shake.
2. Drop pieces into a well-greased Bundt pan. If using nuts and raisins, sprinkle them in and among the biscuit pieces.
3. Melt butter and light brown sugar over medium heat then boil for 1 minute. Pour over biscuits.
4. Bake at 350 for 35 minutes.
5. Cool for 10 minutes then flip over onto a plate and serve upside down.
6. To eat, everyone pull apart piece by piece

CHEESE SCONES

Kristin Lathrop

3 c. Flour

4 tsp. Baking Powder

2 oz. Cold Butter , Chopped

1 c. Milk

1/2 tsp. Salt

1 c. Grated Cheese

1/4 Cayenne Pepper

Bake at 375 degrees F. for like 15-20 minutes.

Makes 1 Dozen

1. Sift Flour & Baking Powder ;
2. Add Salt & Pepper .
3. Rub in Butter, add Grated Cheese.
4. Mix in Milk to Soft Dough. Don't over mix .
5. Pat out 3/4 inch.
6. Cut into Squares or whatever shape you like..
7. Add cheese on top the last 30 seconds in the microwave!

ZUCCHINI BREAD

Kim Robinson Fox   *Conover, NC*

2 cups zucchini, grated

3 eggs

1 cup evoo (extra virgin olive oil)

2 cups sugar

1 teaspoon vanilla

1 teaspoon baking soda

1 teaspoon salt

1 teaspoon cinnamon

¼ teaspoon baking powder

1 cup chopped nuts

3 cups all purpose flour

3   big mixing bowls

Please do not over stir these ingredients:

Preheat oven to 350 degrees!

1. In bowl, beat eggs until they are foamy.
2. Add evoo, sugar, vanilla and then zucchini.
3. In second bowl, mix together dry ingredients: flour, baking soda, baking powder, salt, cinnamon, and nuts.
4. Slowly pour the dry ingredients in to the bowl of wet ingredients and mix lightly but well.

5. Place in 2 greased bread pans and bake at 350 for an hour or until done.
6. (When a toothpick is inserted and comes out clean, the bread is done)
7. Cool 10 minutes in pan before inverting them onto the cooling rack.

Note: may be frozen when cooled

BEER BREAD

Normal-sized loaf pan

2 cups of self-rising flour

2 tbsp of sugar

1 bottle/can of beer

1. Mix together.
2. Pour into greased bread pan
3. Place into preheated 350*F oven for 35-40 minutes

Optional: you can melt butter on top when done

Serve hot or cold....delicious!

Fiber

Fiber is the structural part of the plant that humans cannot digest. There are two types of fiber soluble & insoluble-- that make up the Total Fiber. Both serve important functions in our diet.

Researchers & Health Professionals indicate that _Insoluble Fiber_ may be beneficial for constipation, prevention of colon cancer & slowing the absorption of glucose. Insoluble Fiber is found in vegetables, wheat and cereals.

Soluble Fiber which is found fruits, oats, barley and legumes is believed to be beneficial for lowering cholesterol, slowing the absorption of glucose.

For patients with Complex Regional Pain Syndrome (CRPS) or any other medical condition that slows the Digestive System.. or that it's necessary to take medications with side effects that have the potential to create blockages, this can play an important role.

You'll want to incorporate these changes slowly, especially with the Soluble fiber. The foods on your soluble fiber list are the ones that tend to release gases into your digestive track as they are broken down. This can cause flatulence and irritation of other digestive conditions such as Hiatal Hernias & GERD. Making a change too quickly can cause severe discomfort.

Grains	Serving Size	Total Fiber (g)	Soluble Fiber (g)
Barley, cooled	1/2 cup	4	1
Bulgur, cooked	1/2 cup	4	1
Spaghetti Noodles	1 cup	2	1
Spaghetti Noodles, whole wheat	1 cup	4	1
Wheat Germ, ready-to-eat	1/4 cup	4	1
Bran, Wheat, dry	1/4 cup	6	Trace
Cracked Wheat, cooked	1/2 cup	3	Trace
Multigrain or Granola Bread	1 slice	2	Trace
Rice, Brown, cooked	1/2 cup	2	Trace
White Bread	1 slice	1	Trace
Whole Wheat Bread	1 slice	2	Trace

Legumes & Nuts	Serving Size	Total Fiber (g)	Soluble Fiber (g)
Lentils, cooked	1/2 cup	8	1
Pigeon Peas, cooked	1/2 cup	6	1
Green Peas, cooked	1/2 cup	4	1
Peanuts, dry roasted	1/4 cup	3	1
Navy Beans	1/2 cup	6	2
Lima Beans	1/2 cup	7	3
Beans, baked	1/2 cup	6	3
Kidney Beans	1/2 cup	6	3
Walnuts	1/4 cup	2	Trace
Filberts, raw	10 nuts	1	Trace

Fruits	Serving Size	Total Fiber (g)	Soluble Fiber (g)
Apple, fresh	1 medium	4	1
Strawberries, fresh	1 cup	4	1
Apricot, fresh	3 fruits	3	1
Banana, fresh	1 medium	3	1
Orange, fresh	1 medium	3	1
Apricot, dried	5 half	2	1
Peach, fresh	1 medium	2	1
Plum, dried	3 fruits	2	1
Grapefruit	1/2 medium	1	1
Plum, fresh	5 small	4	2
Pear, fresh	1 large	5	3
Blueberries, fresh	1 cup	4	Trace
Cherries, fresh	10 fruits	2	Trace
Dates	3 fruits	2	Trace
Raisins	1/4 medium	2	Trace
Cantaloupe	1/4 medium	1	Trace
Grapes, fresh without seeds	20 fruits	1	Trace
Pineapples, fresh	1/2 cup	1	Trace

Fiber Content of Selected Foods (source USDA)

Vegetables	Serving Size	Total Fiber (g)	Soluble Fiber (g)
Carrots, cooked	1/2 cup	3	1
Potato, baked with skin	1 medium	3	1
Spinach, cooked	1/2 cup	3	1
Beans, String	1/2 cup	2	1
Cabbage, cooked	1/2 cup	2	1
Sweet Potato, cooked	1/2 medium	2	1
Turnip, cooked	1/2 cup	2	1
Broccoli. Cooked	1/2 cup	1	1
Kale, cooked	1/2 cup		1
Zucchini, cooked	1/2 cup	1	1
Parsnips, cooked	1/2 cup	4	2
Brussels Sprouts, cooked	1/2 cup	3	2
Squash, Winter, cooked	1/2 cup	3	2
Cauliflower, cooked	1/2 cup	2	Trace
Corn, cooked	1/2 cup	2	Trace
Squash, Summer, cooked	1/2 cup	1	Trace
Tomato, raw	1 medium	1	Trace

"Some great tricks for making fresh greens more palatable and much more enjoyable:

Wash and prepare the greens, by cutting the greens into desired size and cut off woody stems.
Put the greens in a big plastic bag (a shopping bag will do).
Then sprinkle a little balsamic vinegar into the bag.
Give the bag a good shake to distribute the balsamic vinegar.
Then put the greens in the fridge for at least an hour or overnight.

This predigests some of the bitterness. The trick is to use just a touch of the balsamic vinegar; you're not dressing it for salad, you're applying a catalyst for a reaction.

After this, a dressing of flax oil and fresh lemon is, (oh my gracious) absolutely wonderful! I know a guy who had sworn off spinach for decades, but when his wife prepared it this way, he handed his plate back for thirds.

I like dressing chard collard, and especially spinach and kale this way."

Isabel ~ (CRPS/-RSD)
RSD/CRPS Research and Development

The preferred ratio of oil and astringent vinegar/lemon in salad dressings is a personal one.

In America, we generally make dressings with 3 parts oil to one part vinegar, while parts of Europe prefer 5 parts oil to one part vinegar.

Put the oil and vinegar or lemon in a bottle and shake before serving. Taste before tossing, and adjust any recipe to suit your preference.

Don't be shy about experimenting. Have fun with it. Adding small pinches of one or two herbs you like, as well as garlic. Give it a shake & a taste...

Even just a pinch of sugar can also help bring out flavors and appeals to some people

SALADS, DRESSINGS, SOUPS

&

SIDE DISHES

CHICKEN & MELON SALAD

Dionetta Hudzinski   Yakima, WA

3 boneless whole chicken breasts

1 cantaloupe cut in cubes/chunks

½ lb black seedless grapes, cut in halves

½ lb asparagus, fresh

1 cup chicken stock (can substitute broth)

½ cup dry white wine (or any wine you have that is dry)

1 clove garlic, crushed

3 tablespoons capers

3 tablespoons shredded parmesan cheese

1. Cut cantaloupe into chunks
2. Halve the grapes
3. Trim asparagus, cut into 2 inch lengths.

4. Place on a cookie sheet, drizzle with olive oil, sprinkle with shredded parmesan cheese.
5. Bake in oven at 350° for about 10 minutes or until tender.
6. Remove from oven and set aside.
7. Combine chicken stock, wine, and garlic in large pan, add the chicken breasts, bring to a boil, reduce heat to simmer about 5 minutes on each side, or until tender and done on the inside.
8. Drain the chicken, place in refrigerator or freezer to cool for 30 min. when cool to touch shred the chicken finely.
9. In a serving bowl - Combine chicken, melon, grapes, asparagus and capers with dressing and serve sprinkled with parmesan cheese.

CHICKEN & MELON SALAD DRESSING

¼ cup lemon juice

¼ cup olive oil

¼ cup dry white wine

1 clove garlic, crushed

1   *combine all ingredients in a jar and shake*

Tips for those in Chronic pain. This recipe can be made in stages over 1-2 days. This keeps very well in the refrigerator.

MOROCCAN CARROT SALAD

Samantha Adcock   Shiloh, NC

Serves 4 to 6

6-7 large carrots, peeled

2 – 3 Tbs sugar

2 shallots, finely chopped

½ tsp salt

Freshly ground black pepper

½ tsp ground cumin

3 Tbs lemon juice

dash cayenne

½ cup minced coriander or parsley

1. Shred or julienne carrots in food processor
2. Place shredded carrots & shallots in medium bowl and toss.
3. Combine the sugar, salt, cumin & cayenne; then add to the carrot mixture & toss
4. Grind a liberal amount of black pepper into bowl.
5. Add the lemon juice and toss again.
6. Let the carrots marinate 1 hour. Sprinkle the salad with the parsley or coriander and serve at room temperature

SEVEN LAYER SALAD

Marla D Brownfield (PondEcho)

1 head iceberg lettuce (Use 1/2 head for 4 servings)
8 oz HELLEMAN'S Mayonnaise--do not substitute!!
12 oz Frozen peas
6-8 Hard boiled eggs
4 Diced (fresh if possible) tomatoes
(Depends on size)
8 oz finely shredded cheddar
1 lb Crispy bacon

1. Size your bowl according to number of portions you intend to serve.
2. Clean lettuce well and tear into bite sized pieces. Drying not necessary.
3. Fill bowl about 2/3 to top.
4. Completely cover the lettuce with a layer of mayo so you no longer see green, but not more than 1/8 inch.
5. Rinse peas but do not let them unfreeze and cover the mayonnaise so you no longer see white but the peas are not doubled.
6. Cover the peas with eggs, finely diced, then the tomatoes, again just so the color is no longer showing.
7. Apply a thick layer of cheese, covering with crispy, finely chopped fresh bacon Cover and let set overnight when the juice from the tomatoes, peas, mayo and lettuce marinate.

1-2-3- FRUIT SALAD

Brenda Lewis   *Springdale, AR*

> 1 large can Comstock Peach Pie Filling
> 1 Can Pineapple (chunks)
> 1 large can Peaches (sliced)
> 2 cans Tropical Fruit Salad (Del Monte)
> 1 large tub frozen Strawberries (sliced & thawed)
> 1 small can Mandarin Oranges (optional)
> ½ cup-1cup chopped Bananas

1. I drain some of the juice it's up to you.
2. Mix all ingredients together in a large bowl, chill & serve.
3. Makes a Big Bowl, I put mine in the large Crock Pot it has a lid.

APPLE SAUCE

Kerry Adams, Easthampton, Massachusetts,

4 apples, cut, cored, peeled
3/4 cups water
1/4 cup sugar (I used half white, half brown)
1/2 tsp cinnamon

Put in a pan, cover, and medium heat for 15 minutes or until apples are soft enough to mash....then mash when cool!

VERY easy and SO yummy!

SANDRA'S HEALTHY HEMP CARROT SALAD

Sandra Martineau   *Canada*

Serves 4 to 6

1 1/2 pounds carrots, peeled, halved lengthwise, and cut into 2-inch pieces (halve pieces again if thick), steamed to preserve nutrients

1/8 - 1/4 cup hemp heart, 1/2 of them added after carrots are cooked (found in health food stores) can be replaced with various types of chopped nuts.

sea salt and ground pepper

1/4 cup dehydrated/dried cranberries (can be replace with raisins)

3 tablespoons lemon juice (from 1 lemon or liquid lemon)

2 garlic cloves, mashed into a paste

1/4 teaspoon ground cumin

1/2 teaspoon paprika

1/4 teaspoon ground cinnamon

1/8 teaspoon ground cayenne pepper

2 tablespoons hemp oil (or extra-virgin olive oil)

1/8 - 1/4 cup fresh cilantro leaves

This makes a yummy carrot salad dish that is sure to please and it is stoked full of vitamins and nutrients for CRPS patients.

STRAWBERRY WALNUT SALAD

Paulette Anderson   *Pennsylvania,*

Monongahela Valley RSD Support Group of SW, Pa

Romaine lettuce – 2 heads (leaves torn)
Strawberries (sliced)
Monterey Jack Cheese – shredded
Walnuts – chopped

1. Mix lettuce, strawberries and walnuts
2. Just before serving add the cheese and then the dressing, mix well.

STRAWBERRY WALNUT SALAD DRESSING

½ cup veg. oil
1/3 cup sugar
¼ cup apple cider vinegar
1 clove garlic minced
¼ tsp. salt
Pinch pepper
Paprika

1. Place all ingredients into a jar with a lid and shake well.

Note: added diced chicken to this and have also used pecans in place of walnuts. Both work well. I have also added cucumbers, peppers and etc, and it still is good.

GRACES CHICKEN WALNUT SALAD

Grace W. Allen Weems, Virginia, Now Resting in Heaven

Recipe submitted with love by granddaughter Kelly Allen

4-6 servings

3 to 4pounds of cooked chopped chicken meat

1 Tbsp salt

1½ Cups Mayonnaise

½ Cup Walnuts

½ Cup celery

1 tsp tarragon

2 tsp Celery Salt

1. Combine all ingredients
2. *Let chill for 30 minutes. Serve with crackers or* bread.

Tips for Making Greens More Palatable

Isabel: RSD/CRPS Research and Development

For those dark greens and also for any brassicas (Cabbage, broccoli, cauliflower, Brussels Sprouts), here's another gem:

- Put the washed, damp (NOT spin-dried) veggies in a steamer (though I just put them straight in the pan

and watch it like a hawk. I refuse to wash a steamer tray.)
- Toss in about 1 oz of whisky for a whole head of cauliflower or the equivalent.
- Add a bit of water if it's going to steam for more than 4 minutes, which is about when all the booze is cooked off.
- Cover & steam.

This tiny bit of whisky does something magical to the flavor. Makes it sort of smooth and pleasing, also cuts the bitterness, but doesn't change the flavor of the vegetable itself -- still tastes like kale or cauliflower or napa or whatever.

I've also tried this with brandy, gin and vodka. Gin is pretty good with cauliflower, but vodka definitely does not do the trick. Brandy goes better with fruity stuff, but it does help cut the bitterness a little.

I have trouble with the bitter aftertaste of these things I now have to eat tons of, so I'm all about making them palatable.

Here's another recipe, this time for cooked pot greens. This is from my Mom, Jeanne, who was a fan of the late great Julia Child, Paul Prudhomme, and good French cooking generally.

POT GREENS & BACON

Isabel: RSD/CRPS Research and Development

You can use any pot greens for this -- kale, chard, collard, napa, bok choy (though that's so good raw & lightly steamed, I don't know why you'd simmer it), mustard greens, radish greens, beet tops ... etc.

2 strips Bacon

Pot Greens (kale, chard, collard, napa, bok choy, mustard greens, radish greens, beet tops)

Onion (diced)

1/4 cup Cooking Wine or broth (for deglazing)

Chicken Bullion / Base

Carrots (optional)

1. Cook 1-2 strips of bacon in the bottom of a large saucepan.
2. When they are nice and crispy and thoroughly done, take them out and let them drain.
3. Brown an onion nicely, in the bacon fat left in the pan.
4. Slosh a bit of your favorite cooking juice or alcohol onto them and, while the pan sizzles hotly, scrape the stuck bits off the bottom of the pot. (This is what they mean by "deglazing." It's just using cool fluid to make the stuck bits come off the hot pan, so they don't burn and spoil the flavor.)
5. Add good bullion, either chicken or beef. Simmer up a

cup or two for each bag/ bunch of whatever, one cup if you like just a little sauce, more if you want to put it over rice or something.

6. If you like, add some grated carrots to brighten it up and increase the vitamin A content.
7. Toss in your greens, stir them until they're covered with the sauce, and cover.
8. Reduce heat to a low simmer and let them cook for 10-20 minutes, depending on how wilted you like your greens.
9. Crumble the bacon and add it in the last 5 minutes of cooking. This lets the bacon flavor get stronger without totally destroying the crispiness of the bacon.

BALSAMIC VINAIGRETTE

Samantha Adcock   Shiloh, NC

1 Tbs balsamic vinegar
Freshly ground black pepper
1 Tbs water
1 tsp Dijon Mustard
½ tsp salt
2 Tbs olive oil

1. Pour vinegar and water into a small bowl.
2. Add the salt, several grindings of pepper & the mustard, and whisk.
3. Add the olive oil and whisk until smooth

DAIRY-FREE "SOUR CREAM" (MOCK SOUR CREAM) ☼

Amber Wiseman   *Ohio*

Don't be scared by the word Tofu, it is better than it sounds and can be difficult to tell the difference!

> 1 package silk firm Tofu
> 1 T lemon juice
> 1 T oil
> ½ t salt
> ½ t sugar
> **Optional**
> > *¼ c chopped peppers*
> > *2 T chopped black olives*

1. Drain Tofu, then add all ingredients to a food processor. Stir until smooth.
2. Add optional ingredients for extra flavor.

SANTA FE SOUP

Lisa Coan   *Kansas City, MO*

Kansas City Chronic Pain and RSD/CRPS Support Group

> 1   Lb. Lean Ground Beef - Browned
> 1   Onion - Chopped
> 1   Can - Original ROTEL

1   Can - Hot ROTEL (or Original)
1   Can Black Beans - Drained and Rinsed
1   Can Hominy
2   Cans Chicken Broth
1   Lb. Velveeta Cheese (more or less to taste)

1. Brown Beef and Onions.
2. Add Rotel, Beans, Hominy and Chicken Broth.
3. Cook for 15 Minutes.
4. Add Cheese
5. Stir, Warm and Serve

BEANSTEW

Nettan Svensson,   Norrköping, Sweden

Serves 4

1 onion
2 cloves garlic
2 carrots
1 red bell pepper
1 green bell pepper
150 g fresh mushrooms
1 tablespoon olive oil
1 apple
1 teaspoon chili powder
About 300 g of crushed tomatoes, preferably spiced chili
400 g cooked mixed beans
2 tablespoons chopped parsley

1. Peel and chop onion and garlic. Peel and grate the carrots coarsely. Chop peppers. Slice the mushrooms.
2. Fry the onion, garlic, carrot, peppers and mushrooms in oil in a saucepan on a low heat. Stir in the meantime.
3. Peel and core the apple and grate coarsely, stir into the saucepan. Add the chili powder.
4. Let beans drain if they are preserved / in tetra. Pour them and crushed tomatoes to the pan.
5. Let the stew cook with the lid on low heat for 15 minutes.
6. Season with salt. Sprinkle with chopped parsley before serving
7. Serve with bread and lemon water.

BARSZCZ (BEET SOUP)

Dionetta Hudzinski   Yakima, WA

Traditional Polish Favorite

Serves 5-6

8 cups water
1 -2 medium onions – chopped
4 carrots coarsely grated
¼ head coarsely chopped red/purple Cabbage
2 stalks celery chopped
4 medium beets – cooked and peeled and grated
5 pepper corns
1 bay leaf
1 teaspoon salt
¼ teaspoon pepper
1 cup mushrooms sliced (Optional)
1 tablespoon Vinegar
1/3 – ½ cup of pearl barley

1. Cook until the barley is tender about 1 hour.
2. Remove the bay leaf before serving.
3. Serve hot by itself as a hearty soup or can be poured over boiled potatoes.
4. Add a dollop of sour cream to each bowl of soup before serving.

Tip for those with pain- use a food processor to chop and grate the onions, carrots, Cabbage, celery, and beets.

SAUSAGE STEW

Karol Patras   Calera, AL

This dish is easy to make, it doesn't take much to get it together and it is awesome for me because I have CRPS/RSD in my right arm, wrist and hand. I'm right hand dominant, or I should say I used to be. I've had CRPS/RSD since 2005, I was diagnosed with it after having tendonitis (De Quatrain's) surgery on my right wrist.

Unfortunately I was not diagnosed and treated in time for them to begin the much needed therapy and medications, so therefore it spread up my arm. At times my arm, hand and wrist are not functional at all.

I hope everyone tries this dish, it is "YUMMY"

    1 lb. Sausage (large round) cut up into pieces (I used regular or mild)
    1 large onion (diced)

3 tablespoons of olive oil
Garlic powder, salt and pepper (to taste)
1/2 lb. Wide egg noodles
1 large green pepper (diced)
1 large can of diced tomatoes

1. In a Wok (or large skillet) pour in olive oil.
2. When oil is hot, put in onions and green peppers.
3. Sauté for about 5-7 minutes.
4. Add Sausage and continue to Sauté for 10 minutes.
5. While the sausage, onions and peppers are cooking, fill a large pot with water, 1/2 full.
6. Bring to a boil and cook egg noodles until done.
7. When is done, pour in diced tomatoes and cook for an additional 15 minutes.
8. When noodles are done, drain and place into large bowl.
9. Pour Sausage Stew over noodles.
10. Serve in bowls.
11. Takes approximately 45 minutes for entire meal to be ready.

PINTO BEANS

Kim Robinson Fox   Conover, NC

Always use a WOODEN SPOON to stir.
Always add only HOT WATER.

Bag of pinto beans.

1. Check through them for rocks, etc. (yes really)

2. Fill pot half full of water, cook on high until they reach a rolling boil
3. Drain them into a colander to release dirt from them and pot.
4. Put beans back into the same pot and fill it until full.
5. Bring to a boil again, reduce heat to medium and cook until done. Approximately 2-2 1/2 hours.
6. Add HOT water to pot as needed while cooking. Add salt to taste starting with 1 teaspoon.

Most people add fat back for flavor but I don't. Without it, this is a NO fat, high protein dish.

If they're great without it, why add it...

BEER AND CHEESE SOUP

Kathy Crews   Richmond, VA

1-bunch green onions
3-Tbsp. olive oil
3/4-cup bottled roasted red sweet peppers, drained
3/4-cup pale lager or nonalcoholic beer
2-cups refrigerated shredded hash brown potatoes
2-cups milk
8-oz. American cheese, shredded
1/4-tsp. paprika plus additional for sprinkling

1. Slice green onions, separating white and green parts. In Dutch oven over medium heat cook white portion of green onions in 1 tablespoon hot oil under tender.

2. In blender combine red peppers, cooked onion, beer, and 1 cup potatoes; process until smooth. Return to pot. Bring to boiling. Reduce heat. Simmer, uncovered, 5 minutes.
3. Add milk and cheese to pan. Cook and stir over medium heat until cheese is melted and soup is hot (do not boil).
4. In skillet cook remaining potatoes in remaining hot oil over medium-high heat, 8 minutes or until golden, stirring occasionally. Drain on paper towels; sprinkle with paprika.

SHERRIED BARLEY SOUP

Mom Hudzinski's Christmas Eve Soup

Dionetta Hudzinski   Yakima, WA

Serves 5

2 ½ cups sliced mushrooms (if you can get wild mushrooms they are the tastiest)
½ cup chopped onion
1/3 cup butter
1/3 cup flour
20 oz of condensed chicken broth
2 cups water
1/3 – ½ cups pearl barley

1. Sauté mushrooms and onions in butter.
2. Remove with a slotted spoon.
3. Stir flour into butter that is left in the pan, stir over medium heat until brown.

4. Add broth and water stir to let the flour mixture dissolve in the broth/water.
5. Add barley, bring to a boil.
6. Reduce heat; add mushrooms and onions. Stir occasionally.
7. Simmer until the barley is tender about 1 hour. Add more water if the soup is too thick

Add before serving:

1 tablespoon cooking sherry

2 teaspoons Worcestershire sauce

3 tablespoons fresh parsley (1 teaspoon dried)

1/8 teaspoon pepper and salt to taste.

CHICKEN & WILD RICE SOUP

Erin Dasher   Williamsburg, VA

Serves: 6

PREP Time: 40-45 Minutes

2/3 C. Wild Rice
4 1/4 C. Chicken Broth
Black Pepper/Salt (to Season)
1 1/2 C. Mushrooms (sliced)
1/2 C. Onions (chopped)
2 TBSP. Butter
1 1/2 C. Chicken (Cubed) - can used pre cooked rotisserie chicken

1/2 C. Parsley
Bay Leaf
1 C. Celery (Chopped)
1 C. Carrots (Shredded)

1. Combine rice, broth, seasoning, chicken, celery, and carrots in large saucepan. Bring to boil.
2. In a medium skillet sauté mushrooms and onion with the butter for 7-8 minutes until tender.
3. Then combine everything in the saucepan; allow to cook for approximately 15 minutes.

OVEN ROASTED VEGGIES

Patty Burke   FL

1 envelope Lipton® Recipe Secrets Savory Herb with Garlic; or onion soup mix

2 tablespoons Extra Virgin Olive Oil

1 1/2 lbs assorted chopped veggies (sliced zucchini, yellow squash, red and/or green peppers, chopped or baby carrots, chopped celery, mushrooms) I also add chunks of red onion and chopped scallion.

Pre-heat oven to 450.

1. In plastic bag, shake all ingredients until veggies are coated.
2. Empty into 13 by 9 inch baking/roasting pan.

3. Bake 20 minutes or until veggies are tender - stir once.
4. Makes 4 (1/2 cup servings)

If you are grilling, this can also be cooked in aluminum foil on the grill.

SAUTÉED SPINACH

Patty Burke   FL

Serves 6 - 8

This dish can be served alone, as a bed for fish or chicken; a filling for omelets, quiche or crepes; or as a side dish.

    2 tbsp. extra virgin olive oil
    1/2 medium Spanish (red) onion
    1 medium Vidalia (sweet) onion
    3/4 cup mushrooms (coarse chopped)
    1 tbsp. unsalted butter
    2 large garlic cloves, fine chopped
    3 "baby" sweet peppers
    1 fresh lemon, juiced
    6 slices cooked, drained bacon, chopped
    6-8 fresh basil leaves, medium chopped
    1/4 cup toasted pine nuts
    4 tbsp. fresh tarragon leaves, fine chopped
    2 tbsp. lemongrass paste
    2 9-oz. packages fresh baby spinach leaves.

(Optional: 3-4 Roma or sundried tomatoes, 1/4 cup chopped scallion-garnish, 1/4 cup Feta cheese-garnish)

Preparation sequence is important!

1   In a large skillet, at medium heat, add oil
2   Briefly sauté red and white onions.
3   Add mushrooms; cook about 2 minutes.
4   Create space in center of skillet, add butter and garlic.
5   Add sweet peppers to center of skillet, then lemon juice; stir rapidly.
6   Simmer 2 minutes.
7   Add bacon pieces, basil, toasted pine nuts, tarragon, lemongrass paste.
8   Mix well; cook about a minute.
9   Add one package of spinach, folding and mixing until spinach is turning dark and wilting well.
10 Add second package of spinach, again folding and mixing well. (Optional; add tomatoes.)
11   Remove from heat, and put into serving bowl. Add scallion if desired. Sprinkle individual servings with (optional) Feta cheese.

- Goes well with homemade Pesto with Spinach Pasta

HOMEMADE PESTO WITH SPINACH PASTA

Patty Burke   FL

1/3 cup of Extra virgin olive oil
1 package fresh basil tops chopped
1/3 cup pine nuts (can be substituted with walnuts)
2 cloves of fresh crushed garlic
1/2 cup ground parmesan cheese.

1   Cook pasta and drain, toss with pesto, parmesan. cheese.

2   Flavor with salt and fresh ground black pepper.

OVEN-ROASTED CAULIFLOWER

Tonya Brobeck   Lake Stevens, WA

5 to 6 cups cauliflower florets, about 1 1/2 inches in diameter (from 1 medium cauliflower)
1/4 cup extra-virgin olive oil
1 tablespoon sliced garlic
2 tablespoons lemon juice
1 teaspoon salt
1/2 teaspoon black pepper
2 tablespoons grated Parmesan
Chopped chives, for garnish

Preheat the oven to 500 degrees F.

1   Place the cauliflower florets in a large sauté pan or a roasting pan. Drizzle the olive oil over the cauliflower, and season with the garlic, lemon juice, salt and pepper.

2   Place in the oven and cook for 15 minutes, stirring occasionally to ensure even roasting.

3   Remove from the oven and sprinkle with the Parmesan. Garnish with chopped chives. Serve immediately.

SOMETHING SPECIAL - ZUCCHINI

Sharon Romenesko   Sheboygan, WI

2 med. zucchini, diagonally sliced, unpeeled

1 lg. onion, thinly sliced

2 tomatoes, sliced

2 green peppers, sliced

1 cup shredded cheese

Optional: Add pre-cooked chicken and it's a complete meal. I also add chopped up cauliflower and broccoli.

1   In buttered 2 qt. casserole, arrange ½ of the sliced zucchini around sides & bottom.
2   Then add a layer of ½ of the sliced onion, tomato, gr. Pepper, (other veggies) and ½ cup of shredded cheese. Sprinkle with salt and pepper. Repeat starting with zucchini – dot with 1 T. butter.
3   Cover dish tightly.
4   Bake at 375 degrees for 45 – 60 min. Remove from oven, top with remaining cheese.
5   Return to oven for 2 minutes or just long enough for cheese to melt.

PATSY POTATOES

Bernadette Chew   Chico, CA

2lbs frozen shredded cubed potatoes
1tsp salt'
1/2 cup melted butter
1tsp pepper
1/2 cup chopped onion
1 can cream of chicken soup
1 pint sour cream
2 cups grated Cheddar cheese
¾ cup Cornflakes – unfrosted

1. Mix all together...
2. Topping 3/4 corn flakes non frosted 1/4 melted butter
3. Bake at 350°F 45 Minutes

HINTS Use low sodium substitute can soup and do not add any additional salt to the casserole. Make ahead and warm up in a microwave about 1 1/2 min or until cheese is bubbling..

CHEESE HASH BROWNS

Sara Willy Timmons   Saukville, WI

2 lbs Tater tots or hash-browns (Thaw the tater tots first)
1 can cream of mushroom soup

1 pt sour cream
1/3 cup chopped onion
1/4 cup butter
2 cups cheddar cheese
Salt and pepper

1. Bake at 375 oven for 40 minutes.

Mix all ingredients together and put in 9x13 inch greased pan

PARMESAN POTATOES

From the Kitchen of Jane Gonzales

Author of "In the Blink of an Eye ~ My Life with RSDS"

2 - 1 lb. cans of small whole potatoes

½ cup butter

¼ cup grated Parmesan cheese

Preheat Oven to 400°F

1. Open & drain cans of potatoes. Place in 9"x9"x2" in square baking dish.
2. Melt butter in microwave for 30 to 45 seconds. Add to pan of potatoes toss to coat completely. Sprinkle with Parmesan cheese.
3. *Bake uncovered in 400° oven for 30 minutes.*

Summer Squash (yellow) Casserole

Paulette Anderson   PA

Monongahela Valley RSD Support Group of SW, PA

2 small yellow summer squash   diced/sliced

¼ cup chopped onions

½ tsp. salt

1 egg

¼ cup mayonnaise

2 tsp sugar

Pepper to taste

¼ cup shredded cheddar cheese

1 ½ tsp. butter melted

Crushed RITZ crackers. (About 1/2 sleeve divided)

1   Combine ingredients in medium mixing bowl.
2   Spray casserole dish with Pam and pour ingredients in.
3   Bake at 350 degrees for 30 minutes.

SWEET POTATOES DELUXE

Kristin Lathrop

Serves about 6

4 med. sweet potatoes

11/2 tsp salt

3 1/2 T of butter

3 T Sherry wine (optional)

1/2 tsp nutmeg

1/2 C pecans

Brown Sugar and Butter for dotting

1. Scrub potatoes and cook in boiling salted water until tender (20-30min.)
2. Drain and peel while hot, then mash in large bowl of mixer.
3. Add butter, sherry and nutmeg.
4. Whip until fluffy.
5. Place in a buttered 1 1/2 quart casserole and sprinkle top with brown sugar and nuts
6. Dot with butter and bake at 350, brown slightly 25-30 minutes

Quilt Square Designed use in CRPS/RSD Awareness Quilt Project ©2010
CRPS/RSD World of Fire & Ice Graphics™

How do you learn to live with CRPS?

"Adapt... give yourself breaks & modify the way you do things so that you can participate & enjoy yourself while minimizing your discomfort.

We have to pick our battles!

We won't win every skirmish.... but, by using strategy & creativity to set aside the unimportant... and accept that....

We can learn to forgive ourselves & keep moving forward... staying focused on what we CAN do... not on what we can't.

We'll win the important battles... and ultimately... we'll beat the CRPS by not allowing it to consume us." Samantha M. Adcock

There is no medication approved by the Food & Drug Administration (FDA) specifically for treating Complex Regional Pain Syndrome.

Many potentially effective treatments for CRPS are deemed "experimental" and are not covered by most government and private insurance plans. The inability of the patient to obtain effective treatment can result in severe, permanent disability rendering them unable to work

There is no fast track to effective treatment for CRPS patients.

Hope Over Pain Help Solve the Mystery CRPS Ballloons©2011 CRPS/RSD
World of Fire & Ice Graphics

CASSEROLES
&
MAIN COURSES

AUNT MEDORA'S BREAKFAST CASSEROLE

Laurie Paul   *Iverness, FL*

This is a great recipe if you are having company. Holidays (I make this every Christmas) since you can prepare it ahead of time and just put it in the oven. If I make this for company I usually make cinnamon rolls, orange juice, coffee and you are done.

Aluminum Disposable Lasagna Pan

Cooking Spray

   1 large loaf of Bread (white works best)

   1 dozen eggs

   1 quart 1/2 & 1/2

   1 quart milk (whole, 2%, low fat)

   2 cups of Light Cream

   1 lb of rolled breakfast sausage (recommend mild) cooked, drained and crumbled

   Dry Mustard

   3-4 cups of Shredded Cheddar Cheese

NOTE: This dish needs to be prepared the night before you plan to have it so that the ingredients have time to mix together.

1. Spray your pan with the cooking spray, break up the bread (you can cut it up with a knife, break up by hand (I try to get my kids to do this) into the pan and sprinkle some dry mustard over the bread about 2 tsp., sausage and 1/2 the cheddar cheese mix together.
2. In a separate large bowl put your eggs (recommend you whisk before adding anything else) then add the remaining liquids (milk, cream, 1/2 & 1/2). Pour the liquid ingredients over your bread mixture and mix together using a large spoon making sure everything is well mixed together.
3. Put the remaining cheddar cheese on the top of your casserole and cover with aluminum foil. Refrigerate overnight.
4. Preheat oven to 350 degrees place the pan in oven (recommend putting a cookie sheet under your aluminum pan) Bake for 1 1/2 to 2 hours. Take the foil off the top and let the top get a little browned. You can also wait and put the 2nd half of cheese on until this point if you wish either way works. You will know it is done when you see no liquids remaining and it comes out similar to a quiche.

EGG BREAKFAST SANDWICH

Amber Wiseman   OH

Even easier than running to McDonalds, and cheaper as well! This has been a family favorite breakfast for a long time. Fills you more than just your regular cereal.

Can of biscuits

egg(s)

cheese slices

1. Bake biscuits as directed.
2. Put eggs in greased container, pierce the yolk, and cook egg(s) in microwave, 1 egg - 1.5 minutes, 2 eggs - 2 minutes, 4 eggs - 3 minutes.
3. Put eggs into biscuits, add a cheese slice, enjoy!

Try a pre-cooked sausage if you like meat. For an even quicker option, stick an English muffin or bagel in the toaster while the egg is cooking then add the egg and cheese. Or you can make egg burritos using tortilla shells.

To warm them, I put them on top of the egg with shredded cheese.

BREAKFAST BAKE

Sara Willy Timmons   Saukville, WI

Yield: 2 casseroles (6-8 servings each).

4-1/2 cups seasoned croutons

2 cups (8 ounces) shredded cheddar cheese

1 medium onion, chopped

1/4 cup chopped sweet red pepper

1/4 cup chopped green pepper

1 jar (4-1/2 ounces) sliced mushrooms, drained

8 eggs

4 cups milk

1 teaspoon salt

1 teaspoon ground mustard

1/8 teaspoon pepper

1. Sprinkle the croutons, cheese, onion, peppers and mushrooms into two greased 8-in. square baking dishes. In a large bowl, whisk the eggs, milk, salt, mustard and pepper. Slowly pour over vegetables. Sprinkle with bacon.
2. Cover and freeze one casserole for up to 3 months. Bake the second casserole, uncovered, at 350° for 45-50 minutes or until a knife inserted near the center comes out clean.
3. To use frozen casserole: Completely thaw in the refrigerator for 24-36 hours. Remove from the

refrigerator 30 minutes before baking. Bake, uncovered, at 350° for 50-60 minutes or until a knife inserted near the center comes out clean.

TURKEY -N- TUTOR PIE

Joy Horner   Albemarle, NC

1-2- lbs of ground turkey (hamburger or ground chicken works fine too)

1- can of cream of chicken soup (you can use cream of mushroom or celery)

1-bag of tator tots

1- bag of shredded cheese or approx. 5-6 slices of cheese seasoning of choice

You will use a frying pan and a 13x9 baking dish

Pre-heat oven to 425°F

1. Brown the ground turkey & season to choice
2. Drain meat and place in bottom of casserole. dish
3. open can of cream of chicken and spread on top of meat
4. Place cheese on top of the soup layer
5. spread the tator tots on top of the cheese layer
6. you may sprinkle some spice on the tator tots if you like
7. Place the dish in the oven for approx. 30 min. or until the tators are golden brown.

CHICKEN AND PEAS WITH EGG NOODLES

Suzanne Stewart

8 ounce package wide egg noodles

1 10-ounce package frozen baby peas

1 14½ ounce can Italian-Style stewed tomatoes

6 ounces skinless, boneless chicken breasts

1 small onion, cut into wedges

¼ teaspoon coarsely ground black pepper

1 Tablespoon olive oil

¼ cup chicken broth

¼ cup whipping cream

Shredded Parmesan cheese

1   Cook pasta according to package directions, adding peas to water with the pasta.
2   Drain pasta and peas, return to saucepan.
3   Meanwhile, place undrained tomatoes in a food processor bowl or blender container. Cover and process until pureed. Set tomatoes aside.
4   Rinse chicken, cut into bite-size pieces.
5   In a large skillet cook chicken, onion, and pepper in hot oil over medium-high heat for 2 to 3 minutes or until chicken is no longer pink.

6   Reduce heat, stir and blended tomatoes and chicken broth. Simmer about 5 minutes or until liquid is reduced by half.

7   Stir in cream; simmer for 2 to 3 minutes more until sauce is desired consistency.

8   Pour sauce over pasta mixture and toss gently to coat. Sprinkle with parmesan cheese. Makes four servings.

CHICKEN & HOMEMADE NOODLES

Paulette Anderson   *Pennsylvania,*

Monongahela Valley RSD Support Group of SW, PA

2 -3 half boneless chicken
1 onion
Salt, pepper
1 Celery stalk *with tops* (chopped)
1/2 teaspoon thyme (fresh is best)
1/4 teaspoon dill
Cream of mushroom soup
Cream of chicken soup
Homemade Noodles or boxed shell pasta

1   Wash, trim & chop onion and celery.

2   Combine ingredients in pressure cooker or medium stock pot; add water covering completely with about 1 inch on top.

3   Cook until chicken falls apart and can be shredded, or use kitchen shears to cut into pieces.

4   While chicken is cooking prepare noodles

5   In large bowl add cubed or shredded chicken, broth formed when cooking chicken, 1 can cream of chicken soup, 1 can cream of mushroom soup, & noodles. (you can also add sour cream if you wish)

6   You can eat this now or place it in a 9 x 13 casserole dish and top with 1 sleeve of crushed Ritz crackers.

7   Dot with butter/oleo/margarine

8   Bake 300 for 15-20 minutes.

HOMEMADE NOODLE DOUGH

5 cups flour

2 TBS Oil

4 Eggs (I use large eggs)

Warm water

2 Tablespoons Chicken Stock from a jar – NOT bouillon cubes

4 cups boiling water

1. Bring 4 cups of water to boil in medium stock pot add chicken stock.

2. Place flour in large mixing bowl

3. Combine eggs & oil in 2 cup measuring cup- whisk/beat this together, add enough lukewarm water to equal 2 cups

4. Make well in center of flour, pour in liquids.. Mix liquid with flour and knead with hands until smooth. If the dough is sticky, dust with flour & work in until smooth.

5. Separate dough into 4 balls. Roll out on a lightly

floured counter or board to pie crust thickness.

6. *Cut into thin noodles or about 1" squares I use a pizza wheel to cut the long strips and then cut again across the dough*
7. *Drop into boiling chicken broth; continue cooking until last ones added have boiled about 15 minutes.*
8. *Remove from broth with a slotted spoon. I save the broth for a little while until I make sure that I have enough liquid when mixing in the soup and the broth from the cooked chicken).*

MIRACLE DISH FANTASIA CASSEROLE LEMON CHICKEN

Paulette Anderson   *Pennsylvania,*

Monongahela Valley RSD Support Group of SW, Pa

30 minutes

1 Whole Chicken

1 Lemon

McCormick's Montreal Chicken Seasoning.

1. Wash chicken, place in dish.
2. Cut the lemon in half and place ½ inside the chicken and squeeze the juice of the other half over the chicken.
3. Salt & Pepper the chicken
4. Coat the chicken with the seasoning.
5. Place lid on casserole and put in the microwave for 30 minutes

EASY CHICKEN PIE

Peggy Lindsay   Louisburg , NC

Serves 6

3 large chicken breasts cooked & cubed

2 deep dish pie crusts

1 can cream of mushroom soup

1/2 stick butter

1/2 can chicken broth

salt & pepper to taste

1   Mix all ingredients in large bowl
2   Pour into uncooked pie crust & top with the other, cut slits in it to breathe.
3   Cook in Preheat oven to 350∘F

PINEAPPLE CHICKEN OVER JASMINE RICE

Grecia Howard

1 can of pineapple chunks (juice packed)
1 to 2 jars of sweet and sour sauce
1 green pepper (sliced thin)
Boneless chicken breast (cut in 1 in pieces)
1/8th tsp SaZon by GOYA con Culantro Y achiote
a pinch of salt
 onion powder
adobe seasoning

Jasmine Rice (prepared per package instructions)

1   Sauté chicken with a tea spoon of olive oil over medium heat.
2   Add salt, onion powder, adobe seasoning, don't over season! *The secret is (SaZon by GOYA con Culantro Y achiote) Spanish seasoning it gives it a great color and flavor.*
3   When the chicken is fully cooked, add green pepper slices, pineapple & 1/2 the pineapple juice.
4   Add Sweet and Sour sauce; reduce heat to low and allow to simmer about 10 min on low until thickened to desired consistency.

Jasmines while rice it has a flowery scent and a clean flavor allowing a sweet blend to sort of marry with the meat.

CHICKEN RICE CASSEROLE

Lesle McGuffey

6-8 Slices Bacon (chopped)

1 Cup Instant Rice (not cooked)

2 -3 Chicken Breast Or 1 Lg Can of Chunked Chicken

1 Cup Water

1 Can Cream of Chicken or Cream of Mushroom soup

Preheat 350 Degrees

1. Mix water and cream of chicken or mushroom together.
2. Lay the chopped bacon into a baking dish.
3. Next, pour rice on top of bacon, then layer either chicken you choose, salt and pepper to taste.
4. Finally, pour the water and soup mixture over the top.
5. Place in oven.
6. Bake at 350 Degrees for 1hr to 1hr 1/2 until chicken and rice is done.

BEEF CASSEROLE

Kim Dunning-Powell   *United Kingdom*

Serves 4

1 lb/ 500 g of best braising steak cut into bit size pieces

2 carrots

2/3 stick of celery

2 leeks

1 tablespoon of vinegar

salt and pepper to taste

Beef stock or 2 beef stock cubes

1 tablespoon of cooking oil

flour

1. Heat oil. when hot, brown meat on all sides
2. Cut the carrots, celery and leeks into slices and place in a casserole dish

3. Add the flour to the meat - enough to absorb all the juices [this looks very lumpy but don't worry it all works out when it is finally cooked]
4. Add the flour coated meat to the vegetables
5. Add the stock, salt and pepper and vinegar
6. Cover and place in the oven at 160c/320f
7. After 1 hour remove from the oven and mix the vegetables and meat together in the casserole dish and return to the oven.

The longer this cooks the better it is and serve with mashed potatoes.

EASY STIR FRY

Dawn Clark   CO

1 lb Chicken Breast (cubed)

2 pkgs Oriental Vegetables with Noodles

Teriyaki (or other preferred flavor) sauce

Crushed Garlic and Pesto to taste.

1. Put about 2 Tbs Olive oil in large frying pan to coat bottom
2. Cook chicken in garlic, pesto, and any other spices you like - I tend to add mint to mine
3. Once done add the Vegetable packages, and pour on Teriyaki sauce (about 1/2 bottle) while stirring to coat.
4. Cover and simmer about 5 minutes

LANCASHIRE HOT POT

Kim Dunning-Powell   *United Kingdom*

Serves 4

4 neck end of lamb chops

2 carrots

1 onion

3 large potatoes

Beef stock cubes

Salt and pepper to taste

You will need a deep cooking pot

1. Chop the carrots and onion into slices
2. Cut 2 potatoes in bit size pieces
3. Cut the 3 potato into scallops
4. Put half the carrots and half the onion into the cooking pot
5. Place 2 chops on top
6. Add the other half of the vegetables
7. Then add the remaining 2 chops
8. Dissolve the stock cubes [if used] in boiling water
9. Add the salt and pepper and stock
10. Place the potato scallops on the top to cover all the meat [more may be required]
11. Place in the oven at 160c for 1 1/2 hours

Serve with Pickled Red Cabbage or any pickle of choice

Tip: *the longer it cooks the better it is and the meat should fall off the bones*

MUSHROOM STYLE POT ROAST

Kim Robinson Fox   *Conover, NC,*

2 to 4 pound Beef Pot Roast

1 can cream of mushroom soup

1 envelope Lipton Onion Soup

3 to 4 potatoes, quartered

1 cup water

For Slow Cooker or Oven Baked

1. Flour as needed, salt and pepper to taste (I just use a small amount)
2. Brown roast on both sides in pan to seal in juices.
3. In crock pot, mix soups and water.
4. Add roast, potatoes, salt and pepper.
5. Cook on high 4 to 5 hours or on medium all day.
6. Remove roast and potatoes from crock pot to a plate.
7. Add enough flour to the soups in the crock pot to make gravy.

Serve the gravy over the meat and potatoes.

SPAGHETTI WITH MEAT SAUCE

Kim Robinson Fox   *Conover, NC*

½ to 1 pound ground beef

1 26 ounce jar of Ragu Sauce

1 14 ounce can of Pasta Style Diced Tomatoes

1 6 ounce can of tomato paste

1 small chopped onion, optional

1 16 ounce box of spaghetti

1   Brown ground beef in a pan and drain grease.
2   In a medium size pot, combine all ingredients **except the spaghetti.**
3   Simmer at least 30 minutes (a couple hours even better)
4   Cook spaghetti according to box directions.
5   Enjoy with salad and garlic bread!   Delicious

EASY STUFFED PEPPERS

Joy Horner   Albemarle, NC

Bell Peppers
Spaghetti sauce
Instant rice
Ground Turkey meat
Parmesan cheese- shredded

Turn your oven on 425

1. While the oven is warming, take your peppers and cut out the top and the inner core/seeds
2. Place the peppers in the oven for approx. 15 min.
3. Brown turkey meat- season to taste with garlic, crushed pepper, etc..
4. Cook rice ..fallow directions per packaging
5. In pan, mix-spaghetti sauce, rice, & turkey meat until warm
6. place mixture into peppers, top with cheese and put back in oven for approx.   15-20 min.

Sometimes this is just a good way to serve spaghetti different-you just leave out the peppers or you can cut them into strips and place the mixture into a casserole dish with the cheese on top

At least they think it is different/ or if you need a budget cutter

MEAT LOAF

Kim Robinson Fox   *Conover, NC*

   1-1/2 pound extra lean hamburger

   1 beaten egg

   1 cup ketchup

   1 teaspoon Worcestershire Sauce

   1 small onion, chopped

   ¾ cup oatmeal or crushed crackers

   1 teaspoon salt

   ¼ teaspoon pepper

1. Preheat oven to 350° F
2. Combine all ingredients in a large mixing bowl.
3. Put in loaf pan or casserole dish and bake 1 hour

TONKATSU CURRY (PORK CUTLET)

Dawn Clark   Colorado,

   Gluttonized (Japanese or Sushi style) Rice, cooked
   Pork Cutlets- thin
   Colden Curry Sauce Mix (purchase in the Asian section),
   I usually get Medium Hot.
   Panko Breading
   Cubed Potatoes and/or other vegetables as desired.

1. Trim fat off the cutlets, bread using egg or milk, then flour, then Panko.
2. Pan fry the cutlets until brown, turning once.
3. Serve cutlet on top of rice, pour Curry Sauce as desired

TONKATSU CURRY SAUCE

1. *Add 2 cups water to the curry cubes, stir occasionally while heating on Medium to completely dissolve the paste.*
2. *Once there are no lumps, lower temperature to simmer.*
3. Optional *Add vegetables as desired*

Note- *Can replace the breaded cutlets with hamburger patties*

COCA COLA® RIBS

Karen Slater   *Winnipeg, MB, Canada*

These ribs are sweet and fall off the bone! I get requests from friends and family to make these for any gathering! So Yummy and really easy to do!

4 lb. (1.8 kg) pork baby back ribs, cut into 2-rib portions (you can use other cuts of ribs as well)

2 liter of Coca Cola (Dr. Pepper & Root Beer can also be used)(do not use diet)

1 cup of water

BBQ sauce (recipe below)

Spices (I use salt, pepper, little Cajun, and roasted red pepper and garlic)

Preheat oven to 250°F

1. Spice ribs and place in roasting pan (it's ok to layer them). Add coca cola until ribs are almost covered.
2. Add cup of water. Cover. Bake for 4-6 hours on low Temp. Remove ribs from roaster.

Now you can finish the ribs 2 different ways.

BBQ- BBQ ribs and baste one side in BBQ sauce flip and baste other side. Only need to BBQ for a few minutes until sauce is nice and hot and gooey!

Or Oven version:

Turn oven up to 350°F

1. Place Ribs on a foiled lined baking sheet. Baste ribs in BBQ sauce and bake for about 10 minutes.
2. Flip ribs and baste again and bake for another additional 10 minutes. Or until BBQ sauce is hot and gooey!

(If you are in a rush you may broil ribs for quicker results but they must be watched as they can burn quickly!)

Adaptations:

Have your butcher (or local grocery store) cut ribs into 2 rib (or 4 rib) portions for you (if cutting is difficult)

If carrying a large roaster is tough, I would suggest using the slow cooker. Then you don't have lift. Again cover ribs with coca cola just to cover and adding 1 cup of water. Cook on low setting about 4-6 hours. And then BBQ or oven bake to finish!

If getting baking sheet out of the oven is a challenge. I would suggest using small casserole dishes and bake them in there.

Or of course using a BBQ requires no lifting of heavy pans.

I am going to include a recipe for coca cola BBQ sauce (See page 24) but you can use your own or store bought BBQ sauce. My family loves

Bullseye™ Sweet and Sticky! Or to spice things up Bullseye™ Cajun!

COCA COLA® THICK BARBECUE SAUCE

> 2 medium onions
>
> 3/4 cup Coca-Cola
>
> 3/4 cup ketchup

2 tablespoons vinegar

2 tablespoons Worcestershire sauce

1/2 teaspoon chili powder

1/2 teaspoon salt

1. Shred or blender-chop onions.
2. Combine all ingredients in sauce pan.
3. Bring to a boil; cover pan; reduce heat and simmer about 45 minutes until sauce is very thick. Stir occasionally. Makes about 2 cups.

ROAST – ZESTY ITALIAN DRESSING

Kim Robinson Fox   *Conover, NC*

2 to 4 pound Beef roast (more or less is okay)
6 whole carrots, cut in half
2 medium onions, quartered
2 or 3 tomatoes, quartered
3 tablespoons Zesty Italian Dressing
1 medium green pepper, cut in rings (optional)
Salt and pepper to taste

1. Brown roast on both sides in pan.
2. Place the roast in the crock pot, add vegetables, salt and pepper.
3. Add ½ to 1 cup water.
4. Cover and cook on high 4 hours or on medium all day.

TIP: Don't take the lid off until you need to check it for being done. Every time the lid is off it takes 20 minutes to get the temperature back to where it was.

LIAN'S FAVORITE SALMON DISH

Lian   Australia

1 Serving

1 single serving salmon filet

1 tablespoon of mustard (I use Dijon),

1/4 teaspoon or 5 turns of a grinder pepper (i like the 4 mix of pepper together, but any will do),

1/4 teaspoon powder nutmeg and

1/2 dill (dry or fresh).

1   Mix well and spread all over salmon.
2   Put salmon in glad bake (parchment paper) and grill for 6-7 min. let stand for 5 min before opening.

Note: If the salmon filet is uneven has a small and a big side, spread mix all over then fold the smaller side over toward the bigger side for more even cooking.

PARMESAN BAKED SALMON

Tonya Brobeck   Lake Stevens, WA,

   1/4 cup KRAFT Real Mayonnaise

   2 Tbsp. KRAFT Grated Parmesan Cheese

   1/8 tsp. ground red pepper (cayenne)

   4 salmon fillets (1 lb.), skins removed

   2 tsp. lemon juice

   10 RITZ Crackers, crushed (about 1/2 cup)

1. HEAT oven to 400°F.
2. MIX mayo, cheese and pepper until well blended.
3. PLACE fish in shallow foil-lined pan; drizzle with lemon juice. Cover with mayo mixture and cracker crumbs.
4. BAKE 12 to 15 min. Or until fish flakes easily with fork.

CRABBIES

Tracy Meyer Morrow

   6 English muffins, cut in half
   1 stick butter
   1 jar Old English cheese spread
   1 1/2 tbsp. mayonnaise
   1/2 tsp. garlic powder
   1/2 tsp. salt
   1/4 tsp. pepper

1 (6 oz.) pkg. crabmeat, thawed & drained of imitation crab

1. Combine butter (softened), cheese spread and mayonnaise.
2. Add garlic powder, salt and pepper and crab meat.
3. Spread mixture on muffin halves and cut each half into fourths.
4. Place on cookie sheet and freeze.
5. When frozen place in plastic bag, keep frozen until needed.
6. Bake at 350 degrees for 15 minutes.
7. This recipe may be made in advance and frozen.

EASY SOLE MEUNIERE

Tonya Brobeck   *Lake Stevens, WA,*

1/2 cup almond flour
sea salt
freshly ground black pepper

4 fresh sole fillets, 3 to 4 oz each

6 Tbsp unsalted grass-fed butter

1 tsp lemon zest

6 Tbsp freshly squeezed lemon juice (2 - 3 lemons)

1 Tbsp minced fresh parsley

1. Preheat the oven to 200° degrees and insert two heat-proof plates.

2. Combine flour, 2 tsp salt, and 1 tsp pepper in a large shallow plate. Pat the sole fillets dry with a paper towel and sprinkle one side with salt.
3. Heat 3 Tbsp of the butter in a large sauté pan or cast-iron skillet over medium heat until it starts to brown.
4. Dredge 2 sole fillets in the seasoned flour on both sides and place in the hot butter.
5. Lower the heat to medium low and cook for 2 minutes. Turn carefully with a metal spatula and cook for 2 minutes on the other side. Remove cooked fillets to warm plate and repeat process with remaining fillets and remaining 3 Tbsp butter.
6. When all fillets are cooked, add lemon juice and rind to pan and stir with a whisk, scraping any browned bits from bottom.
7. Drizzle cooked fish with lemon butter sauce, sprinkle with pepper and parsley.
8. Serve immediately with spinach.

SHRIMP DE JONGHE

Ann BeauregardAllenstown, New Hampshire
Serves 4

2/3C. butter
1/8tsp pepper
2 T. chives
10 jumbo shrimp thawed
1/2 tsp garlic powder or a fresh clove
1 1/2 C thin bacon flavored crackers, crushed

1 In a heavy 2 quart sauce pan, melt butter over medium heat.

2   Stir in chives, garlic, and pepper.

3   Dip shrimp in the mixture and then roll in cracker crumbs.

4   Layer shrimp in 8" square baking dish.

5   Add remaining cracker crumbs to mixture, stir and sprinkle over shrimp.

6   Bake at 350 for 25 to 30 minutes, or until the shrimp is tender.

PIZZA

Dionetta Hudzinski   Yakima, WA

PIZZA DOUGH (MOM HUDZINSKI'S RECIPE)

2 1/4 cups warm water
7 cups flour
2 pkgs active dry yeast
1 teaspoon sugar
1 teaspoon salt
1 / 2 cup olive oil

1. Combine 2 cups warm water and 2 cups flour to make a paste
2. Dissolve 2 pkgs dry yeast in ¼ cup warm water and add 1 teaspoon sugar
3. Add the yeast mixture to the flour and water paste mixture.
4. Add 1 tsp salt and ½ cup olive oil
5. Slowly add 5 cups of flour

6. Mix and knead into a dough that is not sticky (add more flour as needed)
7. Let dough rise about one hour.
8. When ready stretch the dough onto a lightly greased cookie sheet. Pour on the sauce and add your favorite toppings: grated mozzarella cheese, mushrooms, onions, olives, Canadian bacon, sausage etc.

PIZZA SAUCE:

Combine the following ingredients:

3 cups tomato sauce
½ teaspoon oregano
½ teaspoon rosemary
½ teaspoon salt
¼ teaspoon pepper
½ cup olive oil
1 tablespoon butter

Bake in oven at 375° for 30 minutes or until the crust is brown and cheese is melted.

TOMATO AND SPINACH PASTA TOSS

Paulette Anderson   PA

Monongahela Valley RSD Support Group of SW, PA

2 cups penne noodles (I used Campanella™ , you can use the whole small box)
6 cups fresh baby spinach (I used 1/3- 1/2 bag frozen

chopped spinach)
1/2# mild or med. loose Italian sausage, if in link, empty,
14oz Italian diced tomatoes with basil, oregano & garlic (I used 28oz gives more moisture, I don't like it dry) (I added a shake or two of dried hot peppers)
2 tbs. Parmesan cheese
I also have added 1-2 cloves of garlic put thru a press.
1 cup shredded mozzarella cheese.

1. Put pasta on to cook, in skillet cook sausage and garlic, stirring and crumble it.
2. Soon as cooked put in spinach and cook until wilted, stirring (cook until unfrozen and hot)
3. Add diced tomatoes, stir, & cook until hot. If you want a little spice, add a couple shakes of the hot pepper seeds/flakes now (the kind you put on pizza)
4. Sprinkle with Parmesan cheese, Drain the pasta,
5. I cook this in my big deep 14" PH Skillet, after draining the pasta, I add it to the pan and mix well into the tomato/meat/spinach mix.
6. Add shredded cheese. Let cheese melt over top

BROCCOLI, CHEESE & RICE CASSEROLE

Lisa Coan   Kansas City, MO

Kansas City Chronic Pain and RSD/CRPS Support Group

2   Cups Minute Rice™ (Uncooked)
1   Can - Cream of Mushroom Soup
1   Lb. Velveeta™ Cheese

2   Small or 1 Large Frozen Chopped Broccoli
1/2   Cup Butter

1. Cook rice per instructions on box.
2. Combine soup, Velveeta and butter in a saucepan.
3. Cook until blended.
4. Mix together broccoli, rice and sauce.
5. Pour into buttered casserole dish and bake in oven for 25-30 Minutes on 375 oven.

BEST CHEESY BROCCOLI CASSEROLE

Sonja Leigh Comb   KY

This casserole is very easy to make. I came up with it by using things I had in the kitchen.

This can feed a pretty big crowd if you have lots of guests or you can make it when you're having a good day, cover it, and refrigerate and it keeps for a week. So you can pull it out and heat it in the microwave on a bad day when you don't feel like cooking. You can also add pre-cooked chicken or ham to it. This is the basic recipe you can modify to make it your own.

1/2 cup whole or 2 percent milk

3 cups of water

1 brick of Velveeta cheese,

1/4 pound fresh washed broccoli

1 box of spiral or macaroni pasta

1 1/2 stick of butter

Non-stick cooking spray

1 bag of shredded cheese

one bag of plain or original flavor lays chips

preheat oven to 375 degrees

1. Bring 3 cups of water to a boil in large kettle
2. add pasta stirring occasionally until pasta is tender; drain, return to kettle
3. Add pasta, milk, butter, Velveeta, stir well.
4. finely chop your broccoli so the pieces are no bigger than 1/2 inch
5. Add broccoli to pasta mixture,
6. Pour broccoli/pasta into casserole dish into prepared 11 x 13" baking dish
7. Cut small slice in bag of potato chips to allow air to escape, then use using a rolling pin or to crush the chips.
8. Mix 1/2 bag of crushed lays chips with a stick of melted butter
9. add your chip mixture to the top of your broccoli/pasta mixture
10. bake for 20-30 minutes
11. Remove from oven add entire bag of shredded cheese layering across top
12. return it to the oven for about 8-10 minutes
13. Remove and let stand for 20 minutes or until cool, cut into slices and serve Yields 12-16 servings

SQUASH CASSEROLE

Kim Robinson Fox   Conover, NC

    2 pounds yellow squash
    1 onion, chopped
    1 green pepper, chopped (optional)
    1 carrot, grated
    1 package herb stuffing mix
    1 stick margarine
    1 can cream of chicken OR cream of mushroom soup

1   Cook squash, onion, green pepper (if using), and carrot in small amount of water for 10 minutes or until tender; drain.
2   Melt margarine in large casserole dish. Add stuffing and stir.
3   Divide mixture in half and set half aside.
4   Add vegetables and undiluted soup to remaining stuffing in casserole dish, mix well.
5   Top with remaining stuffing mix.
6   Bake uncovered at 375 for approximately 30 minutes.

EASY CHILI BURRITO BAKE

Maria Anne Tripp Martinez San Antonio, TX

    Refried Beans
    Shredded Cheese
    Chili (canned or homemade)
    Flour tortilla shells

1. Take flour tortillas, fill with refried beans and any kind of cheese.
2. Roll burrito style and put into a baking pan.
3. Cover with Chili.
4. Add more cheese on top.
5. Cover with foil.
6. Bake until all the ingredients are hot.

Options: *Add your favorite toppings: Sour cream (or Mock Sour Cream)*

BAKED POTATO PIZZA

Laurie Paul   Iverness, FL

Use any kind of pizza crust you like, you can buy it from a local Pizzeria, some bakery's sell it or you can buy the rolled ones that Pillsbury® makes and you can find in the same area of the grocery store as you do for the biscuits.

Baked Potatoes (I usually make then the day before since they are easier to peel when they cool) Peeled and Sliced

1 Jar of Ragu® Cheese Sauce

1 8 oz bag of Shredded Cheddar Cheese (I use mild but you can use whatever is your preference)

1/2 lb bacon cooked, cooled and cut up

Pizza Stone works well but you can use whatever you have.

1. Prepare your crust and put into a preheated oven set at 350° F for about 5-9 minutes to start baking. If you use a pizza stone place it in the oven while you are preheating to start getting the stone hot.
2. Take the crust out of the oven and put the jar of cheese sauce on the pizza crust spreading out evenly
3. Put your sliced baked potatoes then your cooked bacon
4. Cover with your shredded cheddar cheese
5. Place back into the oven for another 20-30 minutes until the crust is golden brown and the toppings are hot and melting.

SWEET POTATO CASSEROLE

Kim Robinson Fox   Conover, NC

1 29 ounce can of sweet potatoes
½ cup white sugar
2 egg whites
½ cup evaporated milk (may use regular milk)
¾ stick margarine
½ teaspoon cinnamon
½ teaspoon nutmeg (optional)

1. Drain juice from sweet potatoes, put in bowl and mash.
2. Add all other ingredients and mix well with mixer 1 to 2 minutes.
3. Pour into casserole dish and bake 25 to 30 minutes at 400 degrees.
4. Remove from oven and add topping.

SWEET POTATO CASSEROLE TOPPING

¾ cup corn flakes cereal, crushed

½ cup brown sugar, packed in cup

¾ stick margarine, melted

1   *Melt margarine, stir in sugar and corn flakes, and mix well.*
2   *Spread evenly over potatoes.*
3   *Bake 10 minutes more at 400 degrees.*

Civil War to ? US Flag Trio CRPS/ RSD[©2011]
CRPS/RSD Awareness World of Fire & Ice Graphics

Complex Regional Pain Syndrome (CRPS) was first documented in the United States during the Civil War. It was named Causalgia due to the intense burning pain suffered by soldiers long after the pain from the healed wound should have diminished.

The name has changed many times over the years, but, regrettably there is still no cure. Nor, is there an effective treatment for all patients with the condition.

Today, our wounded servicemen and women still struggle to obtain effective medical care. While navigating the complexities of the military veterans' affairs system, they soon discover that CRPS doesn't have a specific rating in the Veterans Affairs Schedule for Rating Disabilities (VASRD).

SWEETS
&
TREATS

CARMEL CORN

Amber Wiseman   OH

A delicious treat, growing up on a popcorn farm, this was one of my favorites, a sign that fall (and harvest time) was here! Very easy to make, though I recommend extra shaking unless you like popcorn ball-style caramel corn as it tends to clump easily!

1 c. brown sugar

½ c oleo/margarine (margarine)

¼ c. white corn syrup

½ t salt

½ t baking soda

15 cups popped popcorn

1. Combine all ingredients except soda and popcorn, microwave until boiling, then continue cooking for 2 minutes.
2. Stir in soda, pour over popcorn in large microwave container with a lid, place lid and shake the whole thing well.

3. Place into microwave and cook for 1 ½ minutes, remove and replace lid and shake, microwave 1 ½ minutes more and repeat shaking.
4. Let cool and enjoy.

MRS. CLAUS CLUSTER'S

Sara Willy Timmons   Saukville, WI

1 14 oz can sweetened condensed milk

1 11 oz package dove milk or dark chocolate gifts

1 9.5 ox package M&M's mini milk chocolate candies reserve some

2 cups chopped snickers brand miniatures

1 12 cups mini marshmallows

1/2 cup unsalted peanuts

1   Combine the sweetened condensed milk and unwrapped dove chocolate gifts in a microwave proof bowl.
2   Melt together for 1 1/2 minutes.
3   Cool slightly then add marshmallows, peanuts, M&M's and chopped Snickers.
4   Drop heaping spoonfuls of mixture onto wax paper, then sprinkle on M&M's and let set to harden.
5   Refrigerate to speed up the hardening.
6   Makes approximately 3 dozen clusters

EASY FUDGE

Cyndi Wilson Ellis   Cincinnati, Ohio

RSD Painfree

NO COOKING..... MY FAVORITE KIND..!!!

3 and ½ cups of powdered sugar

½ cup of Hersey's cocoa powder

1 tsp salt

1 tsp real vanilla

1 12 ounce package of good choc chips

¼ cup milk.

½ cup butter

1. Mix powdered sugar, cocoa powder and salt together
2. Cut up butter into pieces and put into powder mixture
3. Microwave for 1 minute.
4. Mix together well
5. Add milk and vanilla and stir again
6. Add chocolate chips to mixture stirring them into the mixture
7. Microwave for another minute...
8. Stir again and you may have to microwave for another minute... not too much or it gets hard.
9. You want the mixture to be shiny and smooth....

10. Pour into a greased 9X9 greased pan.... I use Pam butter flavored and put in the fridge...

I usually cut mine with a pizza cutter about an hour later so it's easier to cut.....

TOFFEE CARAMEL CORN

Paulette Anderson   PA

Monongahela Valley RSD Support Group of SW, PA

1 (7 oz.) white corn curls or hulless popcorn (Herr's Hulless Puffen Corn™)

Place Corn Curls in large roaster pan.

Caramel Sauce

In a 2-quart saucepan cook together for 2 minutes:

1/2 lb. butter

1 c. brown sugar

1/2 c. light corn syrup

1. Add 1 teaspoon baking soda to mixture. This will cause mixture to foam, so 2-quart saucepan is necessary.
2. Pour caramel mixture over corn curls and stir until mixed. Place in 250 degree oven for 45 minutes. Stir at least every 10-15 minutes. Remove from oven and BREAK apart.

CRUNCHY FUDGE SANDWICHES

Sara Willy Timmons   Saukville, WI

1 6 ox pkg. (1 cup) Butterscotch chips

1 6 ox pkg. (1 cup) Semi sweet chocolate chips

1/2 cup Peanut butter

4 cups Rice Krispies™ cereal

1 tablespoon Water

1/2 cup Sifted confectioners' sugar

2 tablespoons soft butter or margarine

1. Melt butterscotch chips with peanut butter in a heavy saucepan over very low heat, stirring constantly until well blended. Remove from heat.
2. Add Rice Krispies™ cereal, stirring until well coated with butterscotch mixture. Press half of cereal mixture into buttered 8x8x2 inch pan. Chill in refrigerator while preparing fudge mixture. Set remaining cereal mixture aside.
3. Combine chocolate chips, sugar, butter and water: stir over hot water until chocolate chips melt and mixture is well blended. Spread over chilled cereal mixture. Press in gently. Remove from refrigerator for about 10 minutes before cutting into squares.

BUTTERSCOTCH GOODIES

We call them "Papa's Goodies"

Brenda Lewis   Springdale, AR

   1 bag of Butterscotch chips
   2 Tablespoons of Peanut Butter (we prefer crunchy)
   2 cups Rice Krispies™

1   Melt Butterscotch and Peanut Butter (we use a dbl broiler)
2   Add 2 cups of Rice Krispies™
3   Stir, and drop by tablespoons onto wax paper
4   Fills the house with that butterscotch smell, we love it!
5   Everyone wants' Papa's Goodies!

AMAZING EASY ROCKY ROAD FUDGE

Tiffany Mazza   Massapequa, NY

   1 bag Chocolate chips

   1 Condensed Milk

   2 T butter or margarine

   1 cup raisins

   1 cup peanuts

   1 cup miniature marshmallows

1. Line baking pan with foil; grease lightly.
2. Microwave chips, condensed milk and butter or

margarine in large, microwave-safe bowl on HIGH for 30 seconds than take out and stir. Repeat this over and over again until the chocolate is glossy and melted and smooth. The reason you do it every 30 seconds is so the chocolate doesn't burn.

3. Fold in marshmallows, peanuts and raisins.
4. Press mixture into prepared baking pan.
5. Refrigerate until ready to serve.
6.   Lift from pan; remove foil.
7. Cut into pieces.

FLOUR-FREE COOKIES

Kathy Wiseman

Great for diabetics, as it has much less sugar than your normal cookie, but is still delicious!

½ c melted butter

1 ½ c oatmeal

½ c sugar (or sweetener equivalent)

¼ c. brown sugar

1 t vanilla

1 egg,

 optional: raisins or chocolate chips

1. Preheat oven to 350°F.
2. Mix all ingredients together, chill if the batter is too wet.
3. Drop spoonfuls onto a greased cookie sheet,
4. Bake for 12 to 15 minutes or until lightly browned all over.

POTATO CHIP COOKIES

Sharon Romenesko

2/3 cup Chopped Nuts

4 sticks Oleo/margarine

1 cup Sugar

1 cup Crunched Potato Chips

2 tsp. Vanilla

3 cups Flour

Powdered Sugar

Preheat oven to 350 degrees

Cream oleo/margarine, sugar, vanilla; add flour, potato chips and nuts. Drop by tsp. unto an ungreased cookie sheet.
Bake 10 -15 minutes or until golden brown.

While cookies are still warm, sprinkle with powdered sugar (use a sifter or small strainer).

CHOCOLATE OATMEAL COOKIES

Kim Robinson Fox   Conover, NC

    1 stick margarine

    3 cups sugar

    ½ cup cocoa

    ½ cup milk

    1 teaspoon vanilla

    ½ cup peanut butter

    2 cups oatmeal

1. Melt margarine and add sugar, cocoa, milk, and vanilla.
2. Boil 5 minutes
3. Mix in peanut butter and oatmeal.
4. Spoon on a piece of wax paper.

PEANUT BUTTER BARS

Wendy Marsh   Macon, GA

    1 cup peanut butter

    2 sticks butter or margarine

    3 cups sugar

    4 eggs

2 tsp. vanilla

2 cups self-rising flour

1. Melt together the peanut butter and butter/margarine (in microwave or double boiler.)
2. Mix all other ingredients into the melted peanut butter/butter or margarine mixture.
3. Stir well until smooth.
4. Spray cooking oil (or spread) into a 9x12 baking pan. Bake at 350 degrees for 30-40 minutes. Bars are done when a toothpick is inserted into the middle and comes out clean.

PEANUT BRITTLE BARS

Jen Dwyer   *NC*

Prep:15 min   *Bake: 12 + 12 min*

2 cups all-purpose flour

½ cup packed brown sugar

⅔ cup butter

2 cups cocktail peanuts

1 cup milk chocolate pieces

1 12-oz jar caramel ice cream topping

3 Tbsp all-purpose flour

1. Preheat oven to 350°F. Line a cookie sheet with foil. Grease the foil and set aside.
2. In a medium bowl, stir together the 2 cups of flour and the brown sugar. Using a pastry   blender, cut in butter until mixture is crumbly. Press mixture onto bottom of prepared pan.
3. Bake about 12 minutes or until golden brown.
4. Sprinkle peanuts and milk chocolate pieces over top.
5. In a small bowl, stir together caramel topping and the 3 tablespoons of flour. Drizzle over top.
6. Bake for 12 to 15 minutes more or until caramel is bubbly.
7. Cool on a wire rack. Carefully lift foil, gently peel away from edges. Cut into bars

FUDGE KRINKLES

Kellye Van Dyke   *Crestview, FL*

1 box of SuperMoist™ devil's food cake mix

1/3 cup of vegetable oil

2 eggs

1 teaspoon of vanilla

powder sugar (to roll the chocolate balls in, maybe 1 cup)

1. Heat oven to 350°F, use a nonstick cookie sheet (I line it with aluminum foil just to make clean up easy and to I can make multiple batches)

2. In large bowl, stir dry cake mix, oil, eggs and vanilla.. takes a bit of strength but comes together so easily and soon pulls away from the sides of the bowl into a ball
3. Refrigerate dough (you can or not, I usually do not, my kid is too impatient), Shape into 1 inch balls, then rolls them into the powder sugar (make sure all balls are uniform). Place the cookies onto the cookie sheet 2 inches apart.
4. Bake 9 to 11 minutes according to your oven (they all cook different), Make sure they are not too dry, they will look a little wet in the cracks but that is good and makes them chewy) Cool one minute and remove from cookie sheet.. cool completely, unless you have a greedy family who cannot wait like mine (they love them warm..lol) and store tightly covered

HAYSTACKS

Joy Horner   *Albemarle, NC*

1- bag of Butterscotch chips

Approx. 1/2 bag of Chow Mein Noodles

wax paper or aluminum foil

cooking oil or non-stick spray

1. Lay wax paper or aluminum foil on counter
2. Spray lightly with non-stick cooking spray or lightly cover with oil

3. Pour butterscotch chips into microwave safe bowl (glass works best) microwave butterscotch chips for 1 min- (to see if they are melted get them out and stir them because they may not look melted...if not melted put them back in for 10 sec at a time- stirring in between)
4. When chips are melted, stir in noodles. (you want the noodles to be covered with butterscotch so it is best to add a little at a time until you have a good mixture.
5. Spoon small amounts (like little haystacks) the haystack will be ready to eat when they dry (usually in about 15-30min)

EASY 1, 2, 3, 4 SUGAR -- CHOCOLATE CHIP COOKIES

Brooke Nelson   *VA*

Great recipe for Christmas cookie gift giving and bake event with the kids..!

1 tsp of baking soda

1 tsp of salt

1 tsp of vanilla extract

1 cup (2 sticks) of butter

2 cups of flour

2 eggs

2 cups chocolate chips (optional)

¾ cup of brown sugar

¾ cup of white granulated sugar

1. Preheat oven to 375°F
2. Mix baking soda, salt, and flour in a medium size bowl
3. Combine butter, brown sugar, white sugar, and vanilla
4. Add and mix eggs to the mixture
5. Put flour mixture into the wet mixture in 4 parts stirring each time
6. Add chocolate chips, nuts, or other topping of your choice to the mixture
7. Put 1" balls of the dough on to a pan (Option: use stone which works best)
8. Bake for 10 minutes

NO BAKE COOKIES: RECIPE #1

Suzanne Stewart

2 cups white sugar
1/4 cup unsweetened cocoa powder
1/2 cup milk
1/2 cup butter
1 teaspoon vanilla extract I
1 pinch salt
1/2 cup chunky peanut butter
3 cups quick cooking oats

1. In a saucepan over medium heat, combine the cocoa, sugar, milk and butter. Bring to a boil, stirring occasionally. Boil for 1 minute.

2. Remove from heat and stir in the salt, vanilla, oats and peanut butter.
3. Drop by rounded spoonfuls onto waxed paper. Allow cookies to cool for at least 1 hour

PUNCH BOWL CAKE

Jennifer L. Brande

Here is my recipe for Punch Bowl Cake. This is one of the best desserts of all time. You can make it with or without alcohol. I will send you a picture of it when I can find one.

3 Boxes Chocolate Devils Food Cake Mix

3 Boxes Chocolate Devils Food Pudding

2 Large Tubs of Cool Whip® Topping

6 Packages Heath® Bits (although I have used m&m®'s or other types of small candy as well)

3 cups Coffee Liquor (Kahlua®, Starbucks®, Baileys® or Godiva® works best-This part is optional)

1. Prepare the devil's food cake per the directions on the box. Once cooled, cut into squares for assembly. Set aside.
2. Prepare the devils food pudding according to the directions on the box. Set aside for assembly.
3. Putting together the cake:

4. Layer in this order in the bowl:
5. Devils Food Cake
6. Coffee Liquor, ensuring that it soaks totally into cake- Remember this is optional!
7. Cool Whip
8. Heath Bits
9. Keep layering until you have no more room in the bowl or run out of ingredients.

GUILT FREE CHEESE CAKE ☼

Samantha Adcock   Shiloh, NC

CRPS/RSD Awareness World of Fire & Ice Graphics

Hope Over Pain

Although I personally, don't care for cheesecake, my mother & husband both love it. This is a great treat for Diabetics, and by using a Low or No Fat option of the Cream Cheese it's great for those concerned about the Fat or Carbs in their diet as well.

1 8 oz. block Cream Cheese (softened)

1 1/2 t Splenda®

1 t Vanilla
1 8 oz. Cool Whip®

1 9 inch NILLA® Wafers pie crust

Special Equipment:

- Neoprene Gloves
- Free standing mixer with mixer & paddle attachment.
- Silicon spatula
- Bar stool

Most of you won't need all if any, of the special equipment listed. But, for those of you who, like me developed the "cold" CRPS/RSD. I hope you find them as helpful as I have.

Get a good pair of Neoprene Gloves (SCUBA® gloves are great, but rather cumbersome for anything other than stocking the freezer) for handling cold drinks & reaching into the refrigerator.

Switching to a Free Standing Mixer instead of a hand held will help to eliminate the problem with the Vibration triggering a Pain Spike or an extended Flare.

1   Combine softened cream cheese, vanilla & Splenda® in mixer bowl, set mixer on low slowly blend until smooth using the mixing attachment.
2   Once ingredients are well blended, remove mixing attachment, use silicone spatula to remove all of cream cheese mixture from mixing head, reserve mixture in bowl

3   Attach paddle head & add Cool Whip® allow to mix on lowest setting until well blended, watch carefully & do not allow to over mix.
4   Spoon mixture into preformed Pie Crust, it may overfill crust… that's fine. Smooth with silicone spatula
5   Cover with enclosed cover & chill

Note For best results, prepare the night before or several hours before you plan to serve to allow the flavors to fully meld together.

*"**No Ice:** CRPS patients are often prescribed (repeated) cryotherapy (ice) treatments because it can sometimes numb pain and inflammation temporarily, unfortunately this also damages the nerves and cells, once the freezing wears off you are left with even more pain due to new damage and re-awakening of those nerves, and so the cycle is then repeated, again and again.. We all know that it takes very little to physically hurt CRPS limbs but ice therapy actually damages the cells and nerves of CRPS patients permanently"*

Sandra Martineau (CRPS/RSD) RSD/CRPS Research and Development

PINEAPPLE-CHERRY DUMP CAKE

Amber Wiseman   OH

Do you enjoy pineapple-upside down cake, but don't enjoy the work? This recipe requires no stirring, no measuring, and hardly any work. A delicious dessert with only a few minutes work! Keep ingredients on hand for company or anytime.

20 oz. crushed pineapple in heavy syrup

21 oz. can pie filling

vanilla cake mix

stick of butter

1. Preheat oven to 350°. F
2. Grease a 9" by 14" pan.
3. Spread pineapple with syrup over bottom of the pan.
4. Spoon can of cherry pie filling over the pineapple.
5. Sprinkle the cake mix over the fruit.
6. Slice butter thinly and spread evenly over cake mix.
7. Bake 50 minutes or until golden!

MEXICAN WEDDING CAKES

Bernadette Chew   Chico, CA

1 cup butter (2 cubes)

3/4 cup powdered sugar

2 cup flour

1 teaspoon vanilla

1 cup chopped pecans

1. Mix ingredients in order given.
2. Roll by hand into small balls about 3/4 inch in diameter.
3. Place on ungreased cookie sheet.
4. Bake at 325°F about 30 Min.
5. Roll in powdered sugar while hot.
6. Repeat when cold.
7. Amount 3 dozen.

DAIRY-FREE LEMON CHEESECAKE

Amber Wiseman   OH

This recipe might sound odd if you aren't familiar with Tofu, but when you are done, it is difficult to tell it apart from the real thing!

1 graham cracker crust

2 pkg silk firm Tofu

4 separated eggs

1 c sugar

¼ c lemon juice

2 T flour

1 t vanilla

½ t salt

optional: 1 T grated lemon rind

1. Preheat oven to 350°.
2. Drain Tofu.
3. Use a food processor to beat all ingredients except crust and egg whites. In a separate bowl, whip egg whites until stiff.
4. Combine with remaining ingredients.
5. Add to pie crust.
6. Bake 60 to 65 minutes or until almost firm.
7. Cool before serving.

Tips:

To reduce vibrations, try using a stand mixer instead of a food processor or hand mixer.

Consider cooking as physical or occupational therapy, but enjoy it too!

Gently push yourself a little out of your comfort zone.

Pain in your hands?

Try making peanut butter cookies and rolling them by hand.

In your feet?

Try to stand for a little longer each time you cook.

You may find the cooking distracts you from your pain!

EASY DUMP CAKE

Peggy Lindsay   Louisburg, NC

1 large can crushed pineapple
1 large can cherry pie filling
1 can Angel flake coconut
1box Duncan Hines deluxe yellow cake mix
1 cup chopped pecans
1 stick butter (melted)

1. Preheat oven to 350°F
2. Place first 3 ingredients in buttered 9X13 pan.
3. Spread cake mix on directly from box & press.
4. Pour on melted butter & sprinkle with pecans. Bake in preheated oven 350 degrees for about 1 hour.
5. Dump cake onto cake board or serve as is.

STRAWBERRY PUDDING CAKE

Kim Robinson Fox   Conover, NC

1 pre-packaged angel food cake

1 ½ cup strawberries (you may substitute other fruits)

2 small boxes instant vanilla pudding

3 cups 2% milk

1 eight ounce bowl of cool whip (low-fat or fat free)

1. Mix pudding and milk together, then add cool whip.
2. Tear cake in small pieces.
3. Place half of cake in glass dish.
4. Cover with half of strawberries.
5. Cover strawberries with half of pudding mixture.
6. Repeat 3 layers.
7. Ready to eat!

This is a great LOW FAT dessert!

APPLESAUCE CAKE

Laurie Paul   Iverness, FL

1 Box of graham cracker crumbs
2 TSP brown sugar
2 sticks margarine

1 large jar of store brand apple sauce
Cooking Spray
Square Baking Dish
1 large container of Cool Whip (thawed)

- Prepare the night before you plan to serve this dessert.

Preheat oven to 350° F

1. Melt margarine in a medium sauce pan. Once completely melted, remove from heat. Add brown sugar and enough graham crackers to absorb all the butter so that the graham cracker crumbs stick together.
2. Spray your baking dish then press one layer of graham cracker crumbs(1/3 of the mixture) to the bottom of the pan, pour 1/2 the jar of apple sauce over the graham crackers then put another layer of graham cracker crumbs, then the remaining apple sauce and the balance of the graham cracker crumbs.
3. Place dish into over and bake for 30 minutes. Turn off oven and leave the dish in the oven overnight.
4. The next morning put the pan into the refrigerator for a few hours until chilled. When ready to serve take out of refrigerator take a butter knife and go around the outside of the pan to loosen. Turn upside down onto your serving plate. Cover the entire cake with Cool Whip and serve

QUICK AND EASY RED VELVET CAKE

Wendy Marsh   *Macon, GA*

Extremely Moist & Delicious!!

1/2 box white cake mix

1/2 box German chocolate cake mix

3 eggs

1/4 stick butter or margarine (melted or very soft)

1/4 cup cooking oil

1 cup milk

1 bottle red food coloring

1/2 tsp. vanilla

1 tsp. vinegar

1. Mix all ingredients together at medium speed for 2-3 minutes.

2. Pour into three (3) 9-inch baking pans (oiled and floured.)

3. Bake at 325 degrees for 15-20 minutes or until a toothpick inserted into middle comes out clean.

FROSTING FOR RED VELVET CAKE

1 - 8 oz. pkg. cream cheese at room temperature

1 stick butter or margarine at room temperature

1 box 4x confectioners' sugar

1 tsp. vanilla flavoring

1 cup chopped pecans (if desired)

1. Combine cream cheese, margarine, 4x sugar and vanilla with mixer until creamy. Add

2. chopped nuts (if desired.) Spread evenly between layers, around side of cake and on

3. top. You may decorate top with full 1/2 size pecans (if desired.)

CHOCOLATE CAKE

Tiffany Mazza   Massapequa, NY

2 cups sugar

1-3/4 cups all-purpose flour

3/4 cup HERSHEY'S Cocoa

1-1/2 teaspoons baking powder

1-1/2 teaspoons baking soda

1 teaspoon salt

2 eggs

1 cup milk

1/2 cup vegetable oil

2 teaspoons vanilla extract

1 cup boiling water

There are many ways to use this recipe. When I make it i use a Bundt pan and put a glaze on it of powder sugar and a little water .

NOTE Each has its own baking time, so be sure to follow the directions for the cake style you choose to bake.

1   Heat oven to 350°F. Grease and flour two 9-inch round baking pans or a Bundt pan or muffin pan to make cupcakes.
2   Stir together sugar, flour, cocoa, baking powder, baking soda and salt in large bowl.
3   Add eggs, milk, oil and vanilla; beat on medium speed of mixer 2 minutes. Stir in boiling water (batter will be thin). Pour batter into prepared pans.
4   Bake 30 to 35 minutes or until wooden pick inserted in center comes out clean.
5   Cool 10 minutes; remove from pans to wire racks. Cool completely. Frost with Perfectly Chocolate Chocolate Frosting 10 to 12 servings.

ONE-PAN CAKE: Grease and flour 13x9x2-inch baking pan. Heat oven to 350° F. Pour batter into prepared pan. Bake 35 to 40 minutes. Cool completely. Frost.

THREE LAYER CAKE: Grease and flour three 8-inch round baking pans. Heat oven to 350°F. Pour batter into prepared pans. Bake 30 to 35 minutes. Cool 10 minutes; remove from pans to wire racks. Cool completely. Frost.

BUNDT CAKE: Grease and flour 12-cup Bundt pan. Heat oven to 350°F. Pour batter into prepared pan. Bake 50 to 55 minutes. Cool 15 minutes; remove from pan to wire rack. Cool completely. Frost.

CUPCAKES: Line muffin cups (2-1/2 inches in diameter) with paper bake cups. Heat oven to 350°F. Fill cups 2/3 full with batter. Bake 22 to 25 minutes. Cool completely. Frost. About 30 cupcakes.

PERFECTLY CHOCOLATE CHOCOLATE FROSTING

1/2 cup (1 stick) butter or margarine

2/3 cup HERSHEY'S Cocoa

3 cups powdered sugar

1/3 cup milk

1 teaspoon vanilla extract

1   Melt butter, Stir in cocoa.
2   Alternately add powdered sugar and milk, beating to spreading consistency.
3   Add small amount additional milk, if needed.
4   Stir in vanilla. About 2 cups frosting.

DAD'S SOUTHERN COMFORT® CAKE

Lisa Coan   *Kansas City, MO*

Kansas City Chronic Pain and RSD/CRPS Support Group

My grandfather, John Coppinger, sold Southern Comfort for many, many years and had about half of the US as his territory. He had his own Southern Comfort plane and so many different Southern Comfort items.

We played with Southern Comfort toys as kids growing up. My Dad, John J. Sullivan, came up with this recipe for Southern Comfort cake several years ago (the liquor cooks out) and it has become the most requested dessert at all get-togethers. He has even sold it to restaurants for their dessert menus.

It is easy to prepare and is definitely OUR family's favorite! Enjoy!

1	Pkg of Yellow Cake Mix (with Pudding added)
4	Eggs
1/2	Cup of Oil
1/2	Cup of Water
1/2	Cup of Southern Comfort
1	Cup of Walnuts

1. Mix together.
2. Bake in Bundt pan in oven at 325* for 1 Hour.

SOUTHERN COMFORT GLAZE

Punch holes in Cake for glaze to penetrate.

1/4   Lb. Butter
1/2   Cup Water
1   Cup Sugar
1/2   Cup Southern Comfort

1   Simmer over low-medium heat in saucepan.
2   Pour over Cake.

MINI OREO CHEESECAKE

Amy Kimmel

Serves: 30 Prep Time: 15 Min Cook Time: 20 Min

42 Oreos, 30 left whole and 12 coarsely chopped
2 lb pounds cream cheese
1 c sugar
1 tsp pure vanilla extract
4 large eggs, lightly beaten
1 c sour cream
1/4 tsp salt

Preheat oven to 275° F.

1   Line standard muffin tins with paper liners.
2   Place 1 whole cookie in the bottom of each lined

3   With an electric mixer on medium-high speed, beat cream cheese until smooth, scraping down sides of bowl as needed.

4   Gradually add sugar, and beat until combined.

5   Beat in vanilla.

6   Drizzle in eggs, a bit at a time, beating to combine and scraping down sides of bowl as needed.

7   Beat in sour cream and salt.

8   Stir in chopped cookies by hand.

9   Divide batter evenly among cookie-filled cups, filling each almost to the top.

10   Bake, rotating tins halfway through, until filling is set, about 22 minutes.

11   Transfer tins to wire racks to cool completely.

12   Refrigerate (in tins) at least 4 hours (or up to overnight).

13   Remove from tins just before serving.

CHOCOLATE CHOCOLATE CHIP CAKE

Lisa Coan   *Kansas City, MO*

Kansas City Chronic Pain and RSD/CRPS Support Group

This is one of my very favorite recipes because it is so very simple and doesn't even require a bowl! You mix everything in the pan it is baked in!!! This cake is so delicious and it is almost guaranteed that people will want to know the recipe.

4	Eggs
½	Cup Oil
½	Cup Water
1	Cup Sour Cream
1	14 – 16 oz. Package of Chocolate Chips
1	Duncan Hines Devil's Food Cake Mix (or equivalent)
1	Pkg. Instant Chocolate Pudding (regular size)

1 Grease a 9" X 13" pan.
2 Put oil, water and eggs in the pan and mix together.
3 Mix in remaining ingredients adding the Chocolate Chips last.

Bake at 350 °F for 55-60 minutes.

Sprinkle with powdered sugar after cooling.

KIWI PAVLOVA

Maureen McNamara   Waimate, New Zealand

Favorite dessert in New Zealand, also claimed by Australia. But of course it is the New Zealand Pavlova!

The Kiwi is a flightless bird native to New Zealand; one of New Zealand's icons and why New Zealanders call themselves Kiwis.)

Pavlova is a meringue-based dessert named after the Russian ballet dancer Anna Pavlova.

4 egg whites

2 cups castor or 10XX (confectioners) sugar

2 teaspoon cornstarch

1 teaspoon vanilla extract

1 teaspoon vinegar

1 tablespoon water

Preheat oven to 200°C or 400°F

1. Draw circle on baking paper and place on baking sheet
2. Beat egg whites until stiff (best to use electric mixer to get more air in the egg whites).
3. Gradually add sugar while beating and continue to beat until mixture is thick and shiny.
4. Fold in cornstarch, then vanilla and vinegar
5. Drop or pipe mixture onto prepared paper
6. Lower oven temperature to 100°C or 200°F
7. Place Pav in oven for 1 hour. Turn off oven and leave Pav in for 3 more hours
8. Serve with cream and fruit (looks good with green or gold Kiwi fruit, strawberries or peaches, etc.)

EASY DESSERT

Tammy Broselow

Prepared Cake (store bought or from a mix)

Instant Pudding

Fruit (fresh)

Shredded Coconut

Whipped Cream

Cake/Pudding and then some Dessert!

1. Bake a cake or buy an angel food cake.
2. Cut into squares.
3. Make an instant pudding, flavor of your choice.
4. Cut up your favorite fruits. I like Strawberries, blueberries, pineapple, fresh shredded coconut, all washed and cut up if necessary.
5. Layer into a bowl or a cake dish, whatever dish you favor. Layer Cake, pudding, fruit as many layers as it takes to use what you cut up.
6. Top off with Whipped Cream if you wish.

Yummy easy and ready to eat. Not that many calories depending on how much you eat at one time

APPLE MACAROON PUDDING

Dionetta Hudzinski   Yakima, WA

(SERVES 5-6)

¼ cup flour

½ tsp baking powder

¼ tsp salt

1 egg beaten

¾ cup sugar

5 apples peeled, cored and sliced

5 Tablespoons butter (can use less)

Cinnamon

1 Peel, core and slice apples
2 Arrange apple slices in Deep, well-greased baking dish
3 Sprinkle ¼ cup sugar over Apple slices and dot with butter
4 Mix flour, baking powder, salt in a bowl
5 Beat egg until light and fluffy, add ½ cup sugar and beat well.
6 Add to the flour mixture, mix well.
7 Add 1 tablespoon melted butter to the flour mixture, mix well.
8 Pour mixture evenly over the apple slices
9 Dot with remaining butter & Sprinkle with cinnamon
10 Bake in oven at 370° for 30 -35 minutes or until apples are tender.

For those in pain – do this in stages and rest in between.

MICROWAVE PUDDING

Lesle McGuffey

1 Cup Sugar
1/4 Cup Flour
1 Egg
2 Cups Milk
Pinch of Salt
For Chocolate Add 3 Tbs. Coco

1. Stir all ingredients in large microwave safe dish.
2. Microwave 3 minutes, stir.
3. Repeat 2 more times, stirring after each 3 minute interval.
4. Add 1 Tbs. Butter and 1 tsp. of vanilla.
5. Stir and Enjoy.

APPLESAUCE KUGEL

Stephanie Maberry   Souderton PA

1 pound of wide egg noodles
4 eggs
2 tbsp. sugar
½ tsp. vanilla extract
½ cup melted margarine
2 cups raisins
2 cups chunky applesauce
2 tbsp. Cinnamon and sugar (mixed together)

Cook noodles until nearly tender and drain, set aside.

1   Beat eggs with a fork and add sugar, vanilla, margarine, raisins, applesauce and mix well.
2   Grease large baking dish or casserole dish.
3   Mix noodles into egg mixture, stir well until noodles are fully coated.
4   Pour into baking dish or casserole dish.
5   Sprinkle cinnamon/sugar mix on top.
6   Bake at 350 degrees for 1 hour or until browned on top.
7   Serve warm. Can be a dessert or side dish.

COTTAGE CHEESE JELLO® DESSERT

Donna   Topock, AZ

1-Pint Cottage Cheese-Small Curd

1-3 oz. Pkg. Jello; Any Flavor*

1-15 oz. Can Mandarin Oranges-Drained

1-20oz. Can Chunk Pineapple-Drained

1-8oz. Carton Cool Whip-Thawed

1   In large bowl, combine Jello and cool whip; stir well until completely mixed.
2   Add cottage cheese and fruit to mixture; fold in gently.
3   Cover and refrigerate for two hours before serving....enjoy!!

*I've found Lime Jello tastes the best with this combination of fruits.

STRAWBERRY PIE

Kathy Wiseman   OH

So easy, so delicious! At family gatherings, one of the first things I'm asked is if I brought strawberry pie or not. It is loved by many, and easy to make.

    1 package strawberry Jello®
    ¾ c sugar
    ¼ c cornstarch
    2 c water
    2-3 c strawberries (fresh or frozen)
     pie crust

If needed, bake the pie crust as directed.

1   Boil the water in the microwave.

2   Combine Jello, sugar, and cornstarch.

3   Once water is boiling, add the mix to the water.

4   Stir to dissolve, then microwave for 2 minutes.

5   While cooking, fill pie crust with strawberries (as many or few as you'd like).

6   Once the Jello mix has cooled somewhat, pour over berries into crust.

7   Place in refrigerator until firm.

8   Add whipped cream for a bit of something extra.

BAKED APPLE BETTY

From the Kitchen of Jane Gonzales

Author of *"In the Blink of an Eye ~ My Life with RSDS"*

1 1lb 5oz. can apple pie filling
1 pkg. of 1 layer size spice cake mix
6 tbsp. Butter

1   Spread pie filling in buttered 9x9x2 inch baking pan.

2   Sprinkle cake mix evenly over top of filling.

3   Drizzle top with butter.

4   Bake in moderate oven (350°F) for 40-45 minutes or until top is golden brown. Serve warm with ice cream.

PECAN PIE

Bernadette Chew,   Chico, CA,

Readymade pie crust
2 Eggs
1 cup light corn syrup
1/4 cup sugar
2 Tbs flour
1/4 salt
1 tsp vanilla
1 1/4 cup broken pecans

1   Add all ingredients together spread pecans
2   Mix and pour over the pecans.
3   Bake 375° 40 to 50 minutes in the oven

- Recipe modified for the sugar conscious

CHOCOLATE CHESS PIE

Glenda C, Michigan via her RSD Angel Angie

1 (9 inch) pastry for a 9 inch single crust pie
1 1/2 cups white sugar
3 1/2 tablespoons cocoa
1/2 cup butter, melted
1 (5 ounce) can evaporated milk
2 eggs, beaten
1 teaspoon vanilla extract
3/4 cup chopped pecans

1. Preheat oven to 400 degrees F (200 degrees C)
2. Mix together sugar, cocoa, and melted butter. Stir in evaporated milk, beaten eggs, vanilla, and chopped pecans.
3. Pour nut mixture into unbaked pie shell. Bake for 10 minutes. Reduce heat to 325 degrees F (165 degrees C) and bake for 30 minutes.

RHUBARB CUSTARD PIE

Dionetta Hudzinski   Yakima, WA

Pre-made pie shell

1 1/2 lbs or 3-4 cups Cut Rhubarb

2 eggs

¾ cup sugar

2 Tbs flour

3 Tbs water

1   Cut Rhubarb into thin slices and place in the pie shell (fill to the top)
2   Beat eggs until frothy, set aside
3   In a bowl Mix sugar and flour
4   Add 3 tablespoons water to the sugar and flour mixture
5   Add this mixture to the eggs
6   Pour over the rhubarb and dot with butter
7   Sprinkle with cinnamon
8   Bake in oven at 400° F for 35 - 45 minutes

BUTTERMILK PIE

In memory of my mother in law Vira Lange,

Kellye Van Dyke   Crestview Florida

My mother in law, Vira Lange (who passed last December of complications of MS, gave me this recipe and told me to try it, I hate buttermilk and she knew that and asked me not to turn my nose up to it until I tried it once.. she was right.. I loved it, She is very missed) It taste just like a beautiful custard pie .. easy and perfect!

1 frozen pie shell use a fork around the edges to make it look homemade)

4 tablespoons of Flour (I use self-rising)

2 cups of sugar

½ stick of butter (cut up in slices)

3 eggs

1 cup of buttermilk

2 teaspoons of vanilla

1   Stir all ingredients
2   pour in pie shell
3   bake at preheated 400 degrees F
4   Pie will be all crackly on top when done.

PINEAPPLE PIE

Kim Robinson Fox   Conover, NC

¼ cup Lemon Juice

1 can Eagle Brand condensed milk

1 can (15 oz) of crushed pineapple drained

1 carton (12 oz) of cool whip ~ regular,

fat free or low fat ~ thawed

½ teaspoon vanilla

2 8" graham cracker pie crust shells.

1   Thaw the cool whip ahead of time
2   Stir lemon juice and milk together.
3   Drain and add the pineapple.
4   Add cool whip and vanilla.
5   Mix well and divide evenly into each pie shell.
6   Chill and serve!

SUBSTITUTIONS

INGREDIENT	SUBSTITUTE
1tbsp. cornstarch	2tbsp. flour
1 tbsp. flour	½ tbsp. cornstarch / 2 egg yolks
1 tsp. baking powder	¼ tsp. baking soda +1/2 tsp. cream of tartar
1 cup cake flour	1 cup sifted all- purpose flour-2 tbsp
1 cup self-rising flour	1cup all- purpose flour+1/2 tsp. salt+1tsp Baking powder
1 cup oil	**½ lb. butter or margarine**
1 cup whole milk	½ cup evaporated milk+1/2 cup water
1 cup buttermilk	1 tbsp. lemon juice+ enough milk to equal (1 cup and let stand 5 minutes)
1 cup sour cream	1 cup plain yogurt
1 cup half and half	1 cup evaporated milk
1 tbsp. snipped fresh herbs	1 tsp. dried / ¼ tsp. powdered
1 tsp. dry mustard	2 tsp. prepared mustard
1 tbsp. pumpkin pie spice	½ tsp. cinnamon, ½ tsp. ginger, 1/8tsp.ground allspice 1/8 tsp. nutmeg
½ cup brown sugar	2 tbsp. molasses +1/2 cup sugar
1 cup powdered sugar	1 cup sugar + 1 tsp. cornstarch

LOW FAT SUBSTITUTIONS	
Whole Milk	Skim or Non-fat Milk
Eggs in Baking	
1 whole large egg	2 egg whites
2 whole large egg	3 egg whites or 2 egg + 1 Egg White
Unsweetened baking chocolate	*1/3 cup cocoa plus 2 tsp. butter or margarine for each 1 oz.*
Butter	
On hot vegetables, popcorn	*Butter Buds*
For sautéing	*olive oil*
For sautéing onions & garlic	*chicken broth*

EQUIVALENT MEASUREMENTS
&
WEIGHTS

LIQUID MEASURES

1 gal	4 qt	8 pt	16 cup	128 fl oz	3.79 L
1/2 gal	2 qt	4 pt	8 cup	64 fl oz	1.89L
1/4 gal	1 qt	2 pt	4 cup	32 fl oz	.95 L
		½ qt	1 pt	2 cup	16 fl oz	.47 L
	¼ qt	½ pt	1 cup	8 fl oz	.24 L

DRY MEASURES

1 cup	8 fl oz	16tbsp	48tsp	237ml
¾ cup	6floz	12tbsp	36tsp	177ml
2/3 cup	5 1/3 fl oz	10 2/3tbsp	32tsp	158ml
½ cup	4 fl oz	8tbsp	24tsp	118ml
1/3 cup	2 2/3 fl oz	5 1/3tbsp	16tsp	79ml
¼ cup	2 fl oz	4tbsp	12tsp	59ml
1/8 cup	1floz	2tbsp	6tsp	30ml
		1tbsp	3tsp	15m

RESOURCES
&
SUPPORT GROUPS

CRPS / RSD Awareness World of Fire & Ice Graphics

Descriptions of how it "feels" to live with
RSD/CRPS have been translated into graphic
form in the hope it will help others
understand what it's like to exist in our world.

www.crpsRSDwofig.org
samantha.adcock@crpsrsdwofig.org
On Facebook: www.facebook.com/CPRS.RSD.

Hope Over Pain

100 Catalon Drive
Shiloh, NC 27974
www.HopeOverPain.org
http://www.facebook.com/HopeOverPain

We promote and provide CRPS/RSD Awareness, Education,
Research; and provide support online, via telephone and
via e-mail.

The Here to Help RSD Group is one of
Hope Over Pain's Open forums on
Facebook. We also have a number of
private groups devoted to Awareness
Projects and Support groups facing unique challenges
specific to their sector of our community: Parents with

CRPS Raising Children; Teens with CRPS; Parents of Children with CRPS, Children of CRPSers and a CRPS Joke & Wisecrack Club group as well.

Facebook:
http://www.facebook.com/groups/heretohelprsd/

RSD/CRPS Awareness Quilt
http://www.facebook.com/group.php?gid=146703535349522

Ask Mara
Mara Gerke
421 S 13th Street
Decatur, IN 46733
askmara@gmail.com
www.AskMara.com

Offering chronic pain support via telephone, email, and local meetings, this support includes peer support and coping skills. I have lived with RSD since 1994 and it is important to have support.

KC Chronic Pain Support Group
St. Joseph Medical Center
I-435 and State Line Road
Building 'D' - Community Center
Kansas City, MO 64101

We meet the 1st and 3rd Tuesday evenings of Every Month from 7-9 PM
Contact Information: Lisa Coan - (816) 326-7111
kcchronicpain@yahoo.com

Just a note for you: We originally started in 2007 as a RSD/CRPS support group and along the way decided to branch out and include all types of Chronic Pain. Our group strives to inform, support, connect, inspire, educate, advocate for and give hope to all persons fighting chronic pain, their families, friends and caregivers. I am also the Midwest Regional Manager for the US Pain Foundation and as such, we have backing by the US Pain Foundation, and are listed with US Pain Foundation, American Pain Foundation, RSDHope, and RSDSA, as well as other organizations as a qualified support group.

St. Louis Chronic Pain Support Group
Web Address: www.stlpainsupport.com
Email: info@stlpainsupport.com
Facebook Group: Hope for Chronic Pain
https://www.facebook.com/groups/Hopeforchronicpain/

We are a not for profit group working together to improve the lives of those living with chronic pain

RSD Sisters
Online Support Group
Find them on Facebook

Oklahoma RSD/CRPS Support
Oklahoma City, OK
Founder Tracy Jones
Contact: jonestra@yahoo.com
oklahomarsdcrpssupport.com

Montgomery County RSD Support Group, PA

Stephanie Maberry, Founder

Our organization provides support & resources to RSD/CRPS warriors coping with the physical, emotional and financial stress this devastating condition creates in our lives.

For additional information, please call or text (267) 888-7559, please visit our website www.montcorsdsupport.org
P.O. Box 640571
Souderton PA 18964-0571
(267) 888-7559

Houston Area RSD/CRPS Support

Houston, TX

Our goal is to lift up each other's spirits in times of pain, despair, and loneliness. We will also rejoice when others are pain free and find relief. We will fight for each other while we NEVER give up the fight for ourselves. We know a cure will come.

Contact: Denise 936-336-0800
cleo1406@yahoo.com

"Carers Global Network for the Disabled" (CGND)

Simon Lee Biggs of the UK & Joseph Aquilino of Staten Island, NY, USA (Co-Founders)

Together the two formed a unique partnership allowing them to have operating bases in the United Kingdom as well as in the US. CGND is an organization devoted to is mission to spread awareness & education on a variety of disabling medical conditions, empowering the disabled and their caregivers as they navigate the often treacherous waters of learning to live with a disability.

Like the diseases themselves, their programs recognize no borders, and CGND is determined that everyone effected by a disabling disease, be they the patient, caregiver, medical professional, or a member of the general public will have a greater understanding of what these conditions are, and how we can all make a difference.

To learn more visit one of the CGND (often shortened to "Carers" Websites:
http://carers-for-disabled-people.spruz.com/

 **Military and Veterans with RSD/CRPS**
Provides online support specific to the unique circumstances faced by current and former military, and family members with CRPS and navigating the Veterans and Military Assistance Programs.

vetswithrsd@groups.facebook.com
http://www.facebook.com/groups/vetswithrsd/

RSD/CRPS Doesn't Own Me
www.rsdcrpsdoesntownme.com
rsdcrps@gmail.com

We started off as a dream.
So many patients are disabled and we here wanted to remind not only ourselves but our fellow angels that life is still worth living.

Why we decided to call this organization "RSD/CRPS Doesn't Own ME" is because, yes, we have RSD/CRPS but that doesn't mean that we are less than amazing people. We have goals and we have dreams and no matter what people will try to tell us, we are worth more than gold or silver.

We deserve to wake up each day and smile. We are more than just patients, we are mothers, fathers, daughters, sons, aunts, uncles, nieces, nephews, grandchildren, grandparents, and more greatly we are unique. We are what we allow ourselves to be and if we allow a big bully like RSD/CRPS define who we are, then that is wrong!

We are strong! We walk through fire 24 hours a day 7 days a week, but we are still here. We are still smiling and living life. Albeit a little differently than before, but you can only make coal into a diamond through a lot of heat and pressure!

Our mission is to remind people with RSD/CRPS that life is still worth living. We want to offer support, stories of hope, and encouragement to fellow RSD/CRPS Angels. It is our hope to raise RSD/CRPS awareness that will help others understand the seriousness of this disease.

We are RSD Angels!

A World with CRPS as Your Constant Companion
Samantha M. Adcock©2010

I live in a world with Complex Regional Pain Syndrome (CRPS) as my constant companion. While on deployment to assist the Hurricane Rita recovery effort I contracted an antibiotic resistant (MRSA) bone infection (Osteomyelitis). The Osteomyelitis/MRSA and 2 subsequent surgical procedures resulted in the development CRPS -- also known as Reflex Sympathetic Dystrophy Syndrome (RSD).

Physicians don't know why it develops, but CRPS is a nerve disorder that usually occurs after a traumatic injury, surgery, sprain, fracture, infection or a period of immobilization. CRPS/RSD is said to be the most painful chronic disease that's known today. On the McGill Pain Index it (Causalgia) scores 42 out of 50.

How does that compare to other types of pain and/or chronic pain conditions? Arthritis pain is ranked about 18, Non-terminal Cancer pain at 24 and Chronic Back Pain is at 26. Natural labor and delivery of a 1st child is about 35. With a score of 40, the pain associated with the amputation of a digit is comes closest to matching the intensity or CRPS/RSD.

Now, imagine for a few minutes that we've traded places.

Imagine that this is your new world. You begin and end every day with CRPS as your constant companion.

In your new world... the lightest breeze, touch, vibration, movement or exposure to cold causes excruciating pain. If asked, you couldn't honestly tell someone when you last experienced a pain free day, or when your pain level had dropped below an 8 (on a scale of 1 to 10) for any significant length of time (two hours or more).

In your new world... you know it makes your spouse feel helpless to see you in pain and be unable to help. You force yourself to smile, laugh, and hide the pain as much as possible. You face your friends, family and the rest of the world with your mask firmly in place.

In your new world... you wake up in the morning and are unable to use your hands to sit up—they will no longer support you. In order to get up you have to carefully scoot to the edge; roll off onto the floor, onto your knees—while trying to minimize the vibration to your hands and arm. The fingers on both of your hands are stiff; your dominant hand is locked in a curled position—you now have a claw—the same arm feels as though it has been filled with white-hot coals, while simultaneously soaking in a glacier fed river.

In your new world... when your spouse is home, your 1st cup of coffee in the morning is delivered. You slowly—being as gentle as possible—wrap your hands around it. You're sitting, grasping your coffee cup like a toddler being weaned off a bottle—but, who cares? You know it will loosen up the joints in your hands a bit.

In your new world... Your spouse is gone, so if you want coffee, you have to make it yourself. The question isn't the "no brainer" it used to be. You have to decide if the additional pain will be worth it... and if so, while waiting for it to brew; one hand gets a paraffin bath (dipped in hot wax). Your dominant hand and arm will have to wait until the coffee finishes brewing to get some relief since you wear a pressure garment on it 24/7.

In your new world... while enjoying that 1st cup of coffee, you contemplate the day ahead. For every 10 to 15 minutes spent on a task, it will take 2-3 hours for the pain to return to the pre-exertion level. You've learned that you have to prioritize tasks and pace yourself. You haven't learned to accept your limitations, and will occasionally push yourself further than you should when there's a critical task that must be completed.

In your new world... you've always been fiercely independent, often to a fault. You find it demoralizing to ask for assistance with the tasks that you used to consider trivial, like opening: a straw in a plastic wrapper, a single serving creamer or sweetener, taking the lid off a soda bottle; or zipping up a winter coat.

In your new world... instead of "living" a very active lifestyle, you "exist" in a sedentary world where you need assistance with, or are unable to complete, many of the essential tasks of daily life. Dressing yourself unassisted is quite the challenge, and not always possible. Garments with zippers, snaps, buttons, and hook & eye fasteners have been eliminated from your wardrobe as much as possible.

In your new world... your first concern as you review a menu is what you can eat with little or no assistance. You rarely order anything that can't be cut with a fork because you just can't bring yourself to ask your spouse to cut your meat for you.

In your new world... you're seeking a new doctor to coordinate your care—your current physician isn't on the new insurance provider's list. As you call around attempting to locate a PCP that is experienced treating your condition, the 1st thing you're told is that they won't write prescriptions for pain. Even after telling them that you're fine with that, you're all ready seeing a pain management specialist; they still feel the need to reiterate their position.

In your new world... you've been on numerous medications for the pain, and have experienced a variety debilitating side effects which have included: loss of cognitive function, inability to concentrate, weight gain, dizziness, uncontrollable muscle movement, tremors, hair loss, elevated blood pressure, etc. There are two things that you haven't experienced since CRPS became a part of your life...

1. A night with more than 4 hours of uninterrupted sleep; and

2. A day without pain

In your new world... at an 8 you're breathing your way through the pain, absurdly grateful that you retained some of the Lamaze classes you took 20+ years ago.

In your new world... an 8 ½ is when the pain is so intense you're nauseated and not entirely sure you'll be able to keep yourself from spending a good portion of your time worshiping at the porcelain throne.

In your new world... a 9 is when you force yourself to stay silent, you shift the book you were attempting to read so your face is hidden, tears are streaming down your face, hoping that no one will notice.

In your new world... a 10 is lying on the floor, curled in fetal position, unable to move or speak as tears stream down your face... Knowing that all you can do is lay there and endure. The only alternative is unacceptable. You refuse to give up!

In your new world... it's time for your day to end. You took the sleep aid about 4 hours ago; you're beginning to feel it try to pull you under. You've learned that the frustration of not being able to fall sleep will increase your stress level, making falling asleep more difficult. You lie on the sofa with your back pressed tight against the back; several pillows are wedged around you to prevent your body from shifting during the night. If your position changes, it will cause the pain to flare and wake you up. Your body must have this rest.

In your new world... a brief review of your day flits through your mind as you drift off. You didn't manage to accomplish everything that you wanted to, but completed what had to be done. You still feel a little guilty, but you force the thought away. You need to rest.

Thank you for trading places with me for a little while. While you spent time imaging yourself in my world, I spent my time remembering what it was like to live in yours. My time in your world reminded me that there's still hope. I have hope.

I have hope... that as your return to your world, you'll take with you the understanding that you could substitute Fibromyalgia, Lupus or one of several other chronic pain conditions for CRPS — this would be their world as well.

I have hope... that the next time you encounter someone who lives in my world, that you'll show them compassion, understanding, and kindness.

I have hope... that you remember how difficult it was to put on that mask, to protect family & friends from feeling helpless. To protect them from experiencing the same devastating effects to their sense of self-worth as we have.

I have hope... that you the short time you gifted me with by trading places, is the only time you'll spend here.

I have hope... that you remain healthy, happy and whole.

I have hope... that my world never becomes yours.

The picture in the top left corner was taken shortly before I contracted the infection that began my journey into the World of CRPS. It still amazes me to realize that only 3 years passed between the two images, not 30.

INDEX

Index

Index

About the Author

Samantha Adcock has been a strong supporter of CRPS RSD awareness and understanding since being diagnosed herself in 2008. A quilt being circulated to raise awareness of CRPS prompted Samantha to find a way to participate despite CRPS affecting her dominant hand. With the help of the computer her first foray into graphics led to the creation of CRPS RSD World of Fire and Ice Graphics, a website created to help others understand, through art and education, what it is like to exist in the world of CRPS and RSD.

Prior to being diagnosed with CRPS, Samantha spent over 10 years in the private and public sector interpreting and explaining State and Federal rules and regulations to the general public and members of the regulated community. She is now applying this experience with government agencies and systems to the many challenges posed by living with CRPS. In order to better facilitate this, Hope Over Pain was born, a website whose mission is to reduce and eliminate barriers preventing patients with Chronic and Intractable Pain conditions such as Complex Regional Pain Syndrome (CRPS) formerly known as Reflex Sympathetic Dystrophy (RSD), Fibromyalgia, Lupus & Multiple Sclerosis (MS) from achieving effective Pain Management.

This cookbook is one way Samantha has spearheaded fundraising efforts to support the mission of Hope Over Pain. Volunteers from all over the world have contributed their time, beloved recipes and support to make this cookbook a true reflection of the CRPS community. Proceeds from the sale of this book will enable the continuation of the pursuit of the goals and mission of Hope Over Pain and help CRPS survivors come one step closer to a cure.

100 Catalon Drive
Shiloh, NC 27974

Hope Over Pain

www.HopeOverPain.org
Sam@hopeoverpain.org